play guitar like the great
Singer-Songwriters

Publisher: Lyzy Lusterman

Editor: Adam Perlmutter

Managing Editor: Stephanie Campos-Powell

Copyeditor: E.E. Bradman

Music Proofreader: Mark Althans

Design and Production: Joey Lusterman

Cover Photographs

Joan Armatrading, Eckhard Henkel, Wikimedia

Joan Baez and Bob Dylan, Rowland Scherman, Wikimedia

Bruce Cockburn, Joey Lusterman

John Denver, Wikimedia, RCA Records 1974

Nick Drake Wikimedia, Island Records 1971

Joni Mitchell, Wikimedia, Pino D'Amico 1983

Willie Nelson, Wikimedia, Columbia Records, 1974

John Prine, Scott Newton, Austin City Liamits, 1996

Paul Simon, Bernard Gotfryd, Library of Congress, 1986

Richard Thompson, Paul L. Kovit 1981

Bill Withers, Columbia Records 1976, Wikimedia

Lucinda Williams, Dina Regine, 2009

Neil Young, Pictorial Press Ltd / Alamy Stock Photo

This book was produced by String Letter Publishing, Inc. 941 Marina Way South, Suite E, Richmond, CA 94804 (510) 215-0010; Stringletter.com

contents

Video downloads to accompany the lessons and songs in this book are available at **store.acousticguitar.com/SSW**

introduction

The world of popular music is filled with singer-songwriters who are not just brilliant wordsmiths but also acoustic guitarists with a knack for finding just the right chord patterns, countermelodies, bass lines, and rhythms for their songs. But while these musicians' accompaniments are just as essential to the songs as the lyrics, the skill and craft behind their guitar work is often lost on the general listening public.

In *Play Guitar Like the Great Singer-Songwriters*, a compilation of lessons drawn from *Acoustic Guitar* magazine, writers Adam Levy, Adam Perlmutter, Mac Randall, and Jeffrey Pepper Rodgers bring to light the inner workings of the acoustic guitar playing of 14 celebrated musicians. Organized in alphabetical order, the book covers a wide range of techniques, approaches, and harmonic vocabulary, from the most basic open chords to uncommon extended voicings.

Included in this collection are detailed explanations of the concepts at play in many of the most loved songs popular music history. Among many other things, you'll learn how Bob Dylan approached such tunes as "Blowin' in the Wind" and "It Ain't Me Babe"; the tunings and rhythmic patterns Joni Mitchell used for "Big Yellow Taxi," "Chelsea Morning," and more; and John Denver's fingerpicking takes on "Take Me Home, Country Roads" and "Sunshine on My Shoulders."

Some of the lessons—like those on Willie Nelson, John Prine, Lucinda Williams, and Neil Young—tackle straightforward country and rock fare that's appropriate, both technically and conceptually, for players of all levels. But the book also covers more unusual and demanding approaches for those who have spent more time with the instrument. You'll learn about Nick Drake's penchant for nonstandard tunings on songs like "Fly" and "Which Will"; the intricate, jazz-inspired moves Bruce Cockburn uses on "After the Rain" and "Bardo Rush"; and the surprising blend of jazz and funk heard in Joan Armatrading songs such as "Like Fire" and "Steppin' Out."

Each lesson includes an accompanying video to further illuminate the ideas behind the materials (including Cockburn himself talking about and demonstrating each example!). The videos will all help you gain a better understanding of how to play the music, which is presented in both standard notation and tablature throughout the book.

In spending time in the woodshed with this book, you'll gain an understanding of how the acoustic guitar parts in a treasure trove of folk, country, rock, and R&B songs work. Be sure to check out all of the lessons, even if they seem irrelevant to you, as you just might find a chord voicing that inspires you, or a new approach for generally freshening up your music. And remember that the ultimate goal of this book is to help enhance your acoustic guitar playing, songwriting, and arranging—and to give you an appreciation for the scope of accompaniment possibilities inherent to your instrument.

Notation Guide

Music is a language and, like many languages, has a written form. In order to be literate, one must become familiar with what each character and symbol represent.

Guitarists use several types of notation, including standard notation, tablature, and chord diagrams. Standard notation is a universal system in Western music. Becoming competent with standard notation will allow you to share and play music with almost any other instrument. Tablature is a notation system exclusively for stringed instruments with frets—like guitar and ukulele—that shows you what strings and frets to play to achieve the desired pitches. Chord diagrams use a graphic representation of the fretboard to show chord shapes on fretted instruments. Here's a primer on how to read these types of notation.

STANDARD NOTATION

Standard notation is written on a five-line staff. Notes are written in alphabetical order from A to G. Every time you pass a G note, the sequence of notes repeats, starting with A.

The duration of a note is depicted by note head, stem, and flag. Though the number of beats each note represents will vary depending on the meter, the relations between note durations remain the same: a whole note (o) is double the length of a half note (♩). A half note is double the length of a quarter note (♩). A quarter note is double the length of an eighth note (♪). An eighth note is double the length of a sixteenth note (♬). And so on. You'll notice each time a flag gets added, the note duration halves.

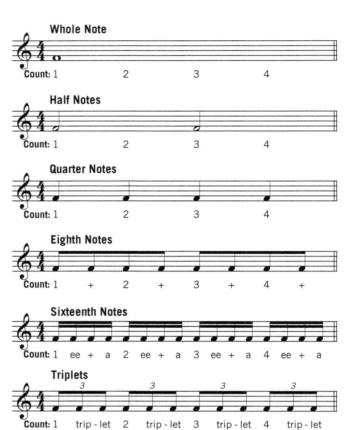

The numbers that follow the clef (4/4, 3/4, 6/8, etc.) or **C** shown at the beginning of a piece of music denote the time signature. The top number tells you how many beats are in each measure, and the bottom number indicates the rhythmic value of each beat (4 equals a quarter note, 8 equals an eighth note, 16 equals a sixteenth note, and 2 equals a half note).

The most common time signature is 4/4, which signifies four quarter notes per measure and is sometimes designated with the symbol **C** (for common time). The symbol **¢** stands for cut time (2/2).

TABLATURE

In tablature, the six horizontal lines represent the six strings of the guitar, low to high, as on the guitar. The numbers refer to fret numbers on the indicated string.

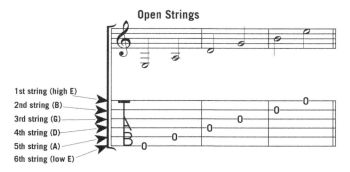

FINGERINGS

Fingerings are indicated with small numbers and letters in the notation. Fretting-hand fingering is expressed as 1 for the index finger, 2 the middle, 3 the ring, 4 the pinky, and *T* the thumb. Picking-hand fingering is conveyed by *i* for the index finger, *m* the middle, *a* the ring, *c* the pinky, and *p* the thumb.

STRUMMING AND PICKING

In music played with a flatpick, downstrokes (toward the floor) and upstrokes (toward the ceiling) are shown as follows. Slashes in the notation and tablature indicate a strum through the previously played chord.

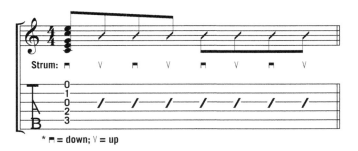

In music played with the pick-hand fingers

In music played with the pick-hand fingers, *split stems* are often used to highlight the division between thumb and fingers. With split stems, notes played by the thumb have stems pointing down, while notes played by the fingers have stems pointing up. If split stems are not used, pick-hand fingerings are usually present. Here is the same fingerpicking pattern shown with and without split stems. Clarity will inform which option is used.

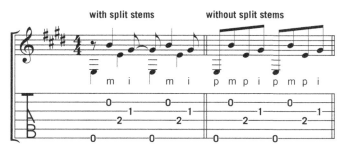

CHORD DIAGRAMS

Chord diagrams are a convenient way of depicting chord shapes. Frets are presented horizontally. The thick top line represents the nut. A fret number to the right of a diagram indicates a chord played higher up the neck (in this case the top horizontal line is thin and the fret number is designated). Strings are shown as vertical lines. The line on the far left represents the sixth (lowest) string, and the line on the far right represents the first (highest) string. Dots mark where the fingers go, and thick horizontal lines illustrate barres. Numbers above the diagram are fretting-hand finger numbers, as used in standard notation.

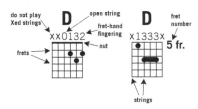

The given fingerings are only suggestions. They are generally what would most typically be considered standard. In context, however, musical passages may benefit from other fingerings for smoothest chord transitions. An X means a string that should be muted or not played; 0 indicates an open string.

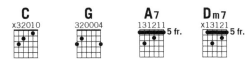

CAPOS

If a capo is used, a Roman numeral designates the fret where the capo should be placed. The standard notation and tablature is written as if the capo were the nut of the guitar. For instance, a tune capoed anywhere up the neck and played using key-of-G chord shapes and fingerings will be written in the key of G. Likewise, open strings held down by the capo are written as open strings.

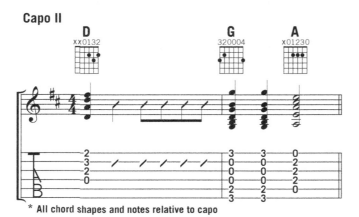

* All chord shapes and notes relative to capo

TUNINGS

Alternate tunings are given from the lowest (sixth) string to the highest (first) string. D A D G B E is standard tuning with the bottom string dropped to D. Standard notation for songs in alternate tunings always reflects the actual pitches of the notes.

VOCAL TUNES

Vocal tunes are sometimes written with a fully tabbed-out introduction and a vocal melody with chord diagrams for the rest of the piece. The tab intro is usually your clue as to which strumming or fingerpicking pattern to use in the rest of the piece. The melody with lyrics underneath is that which is sung by the vocalist. Occasionally, smaller notes are written with the melody to indicate other instruments or the harmony part sung by another vocalist. These are not to be confused with cue notes, which are small notes that express variation in melodies when a section is repeated. Listen to a recording of the piece to get a feel for the guitar accompaniment and to hear the singing if you aren't skilled at reading vocal melodies.

ARTICULATIONS

There are a number of ways you can articulate a note on the guitar. Notes connected with slurs (not to be confused with ties) in the tablature or standard notation are executed with either a hammer-on, pull-off, or slide. Lower notes slurred to higher notes are played as hammer-ons; higher notes slurred to lower notes are played as pull-offs.

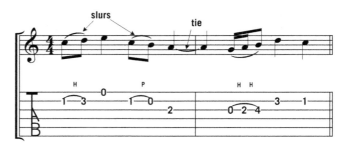

Slides are represented with dashes. A dash preceding a note is a slide into the note from an indefinite point in the direction of the slide; a dash following a note is a slide off the note to an indefinite point in the direction of the slide. For two slurred notes connected with a slide, pick the first note and then slide into the second.

Bends are denoted with upward arrows. Most bends have a specific destination pitch—the number above the bend symbol shows how much the bend raises the pitch: ¼ for a slight bend, ½ for a half step, 1 for a whole step.

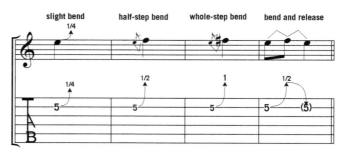

Grace notes are represented by small notes with a slash through the stem in standard notation and with small numbers in the tablature. A grace note is a quick musical ornament with no specific note value leading into a note, most commonly executed as a hammer-on, pull-off, or slide. In the first example below, pluck the note at the fifth fret on the beat, then quickly hammer onto the seventh fret. The second example is executed as a quick pull-off from the second fret to the open string. In the third example, both notes at the fifth fret are played simultaneously (even though it appears that the fourth string at the fifth fret is to be played by itself), then the fourth string, seventh fret is quickly hammered.

HARMONICS

Harmonics are expressed as diamond-shaped notes in the standard notation and a small dot next to the tablature numbers. Natural harmonics are indicated with the text "Harmonics" or "Harm." above the tablature. Harmonics articulated with the picking hand (often called artificial harmonics) include the text "R.H. Harmonics" or "R.H. Harm." above the tab. Picking-hand harmonics are executed by lightly touching the harmonic node (usually 12 frets above the open string or fretted note) with the picking hand index finger and plucking the string with the thumb, ring finger, or pick. For extended phrases played with picking-hand harmonics, the fretted notes are shown in the tab along with instructions to touch the harmonics 12 frets above the notes.

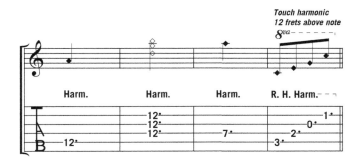

REPEATS

One of the most confusing parts of a musical score can be the navigation symbols, such as repeats, *D.S. al Coda*, *D.C. al Fine*, *To Coda*, etc. Repeat symbols are placed at the beginning and end of the passage to be repeated.

When you encounter a repeat sign, take note of the location of the begin repeat symbol (with the dots to the right of the lines), play until you reach the end repeat symbol (with the dots to the left of the lines). Then go back to the begin repeat sign, and play the section again.

If you find an end repeat only sign, go back to the beginning of the piece and repeat. The next time you get to the end repeat, continue to the next section of the piece unless there is text that specifically indicates to repeat additional times.

A section will often have a different ending after each repeat. The example below includes a first and a second ending. Play until you hit the repeat symbol, return to the begin repeat symbol, and play until you reach the bracketed first ending. Then skip the measures under the bracket and jump immediately to the second ending, and then continue.

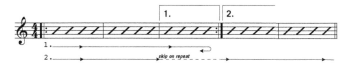

D.S. stands for *dal segno* or "from the sign." When you encounter this indication, advance immediately to the sign (𝄌). *D.S.* is usually accompanied by *al Fine* or *al Coda*. *Fine* indicates the end of a piece. A coda is a final passage near the end of a piece and is indicated with 𝄌. *D.S. al Coda* simply tells you to go back to the sign and continue on until you are instructed to move to the coda, indicated with *To Coda* 𝄌.

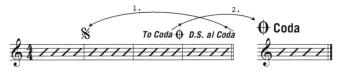

D.C. stands for *da capo* or "from the beginning." Jump to the top of the piece when you encounter this indication.

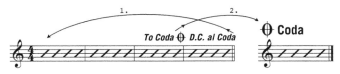

D.C. al Fine tells you to proceed to the beginning and continue until you encounter the *Fine* indicating the end of the piece (ignore the *Fine* the first time through).

Steppin' Out

Inside the Unorthodox Acoustic Style of Joan Armatrading

By Jeffrey Pepper Rodgers

This feature originally appeared in the May/June 2022 issue of Acoustic Guitar *magazine.*

When Joan Armatrading picked up her first guitar from a pawnshop at age 14, she did not follow the typical route of learning the hits of the day—or taking any lessons at all. "That's never been my way," she says. "I would try and do my own songs. So I would make up riffs, and in terms of a chord, you can just play two notes on the guitar and make a nice sound even if you don't know what that is."

That find-your-own-way approach, perhaps, gave the budding songwriter a head start toward developing a sound of her own—as Armatrading certainly did, tapping into the harmonies and grooves of folk, rock, R&B, jazz, and reggae. From her 1970s breakthrough ballad "Love and Affection" to '80s pop anthems like "Drop the Pilot" and "Me Myself I," and onward through her latest release, *Consequences*, Armatrading has followed her own path for 50 years. Along the way she's become of the most revered songwriters of her generation, particularly in the UK, with a stack of awards including a CBE (Commander of the Order of the British Empire) for her contributions to music, charity, and equal rights.

Armatrading considers herself a songwriter first, and her tough yet tender vocals and emotionally incisive lyrics take center stage. But one of the not-so-secret powers behind her music is her instantly identifiable acoustic guitar—at turns delicate, jazzy, fierce, and funky. In the realm of pop/rock, the acoustic is often assigned the limited role of accompanying soft ballads, but in Armatrading's hands, the instrument has no boundaries.

"The reason I think my acoustic style developed in the way that it did was because when I write, I tend to hear lots of things—the bass part, the keyboard bit, some strings, what kind of percussive sound it should be," says Armatrading. "I'm trying to play all those things at once, so my style is quite aggressive."

While generations of fans have felt the power of Armatrading's guitar work, both acoustic and electric, the mechanics of how she plays have not been well documented or widely understood. So in this lesson I take a deep dive into her acoustic style, using a series of examples inspired by some of her best songs. And Armatrading herself, by way of a Zoom interview from her home in England, shares observations about her guitar craft—and the songwriting that ultimately drives it.

In 2014–15, Armatrading undertook what she announced as her last major world tour, and while in California she visited the *Acoustic Guitar* studio to perform three classic songs: "Down to Zero," "Steppin' Out," and "Love and Affection." Excerpts from that session are transcribed in this lesson. Be sure to check out the videos for an up-close look at Armatrading solo, coaxing a band's worth of sound out of her guitar.

FINDING HER GROOVE

Armatrading was born on the island of Saint Kitts, in the West Indies, but moved to Birmingham, England, at age seven. After delving into piano, guitar, and songwriting as a teenager, she made her entrée into a performing arts career in 1970, when she was cast in a touring production of *Hair*. Not only did she love singing and playing guitar in the show, but she connected with a fellow cast member, Pam Nestor, who became co-writer for the songs on Armatrading's first album, *Whatever's for Us,* released in 1972.

A folky production based around acoustic guitar and piano, Armatrading's debut delivered strong songs like the title track and "City Girl." But it was on her self-titled album from 1976 that she fully hit her stride as a songwriter and guitarist—and scored her first hit, with the 12-string-powered "Love and Affection."

By that time, too, Armatrading had discovered Ovation guitars, which have remained core instruments for her ever since. When she was guitar shopping circa 1975, a music store clerk suggested she check out these unique bowl-backed guitars, and she was thrilled to find that their integrated, plug-and-play amplification systems alleviated her frustrations with the crude clip-on acoustic pickups she'd been using. "I tried it and thought, this is perfect," she recalls. "No more rummaging around onstage because the pickup has fallen off or something. And I liked the tone as well."

Early on, Armatrading began to experiment with dropping standard tuning a whole step to D (D G C F A D). While some guitarists use low tunings to better match their vocal range, the primary draw for Armatrading is the tone. "It sounds really good," she says. "I mean, not every song is going to want that tone, or not every song that's played on the guitar wants that register."

"Down to Zero," which kicks off the *Joan Armatrading* album, is one of several songs in this lesson that uses the D-to-D tuning, which gives the guitar a looser, huskier sound. **Example 1** shows the intro rhythm pattern as she it played in her *AG* session,

strumming her Ovation Custom Legend in 3/4 time. Use basic first-position chord shapes except for the Fmaj7#11 in bars 5–7, which you form by holding the bottom of an F barre but leaving the top strings open—a shape she uses in different positions in "Love and Affection" and many other songs. Maintain down-up strumming on the eighth notes throughout; at the end of measure 4, play an up-strum arpeggio that lands on the open sixth string on beat 4, leading to the F chord in the next measure.

While many players would take open chord shapes like these and capo up to play in other keys, Armatrading never does that. Why not use a capo? "I can't do it," she says. "I get confused. I think, 'I don't know what I'm doing here. I'm just playing an E in another place. Why don't I just play the B instead?'" What she describes as a sort of limitation turns out

Tuning: D G C F A D
Example 1 (à la "Down to Zero")

to be a strength, because instead of using a capo to transpose the same shapes, she's developed the facility to travel all around the fretboard.

"Mama Mercy," from 1977's *Show Some Emotion*, is one example of how Armatrading creates propulsive acoustic rhythms with up-the-neck shapes, again on a low-tuned guitar. **Example 2** shows the type of rhythm used during the first part of the verse. Play sliding power chords up the neck—think the Kinks' "You Really Got Me" unplugged—with a spiky rhythm pattern that leaves beat 4 open (with a full band, the drummer hits the snare in that spot). Notice also the two-beat measures (bars 2 and 9) that break up the 4/4 meter and add further momentum.

Example 2 (à la "Mama Mercy")

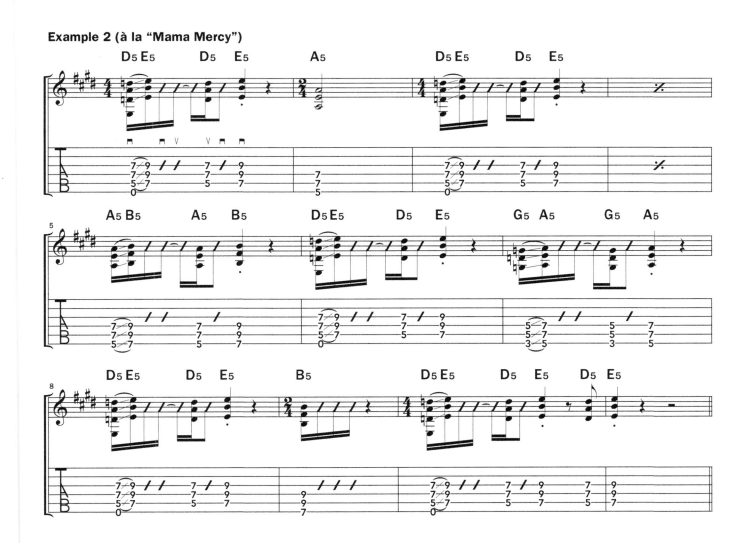

OPEN TUNINGS

While Armatrading generally sticks with standard tuning, she does have some notable open-tuned songs, especially on her early albums. One is "City Girl," from her debut, which is played in open D (D A D F♯ A D) with an opening riff similar to **Example 3**. Pick a bass line by sliding on the fifth string up to the fifth fret in the first measure, and then follow with a walk-up to the A chord.

During her last world tour, Armatrading played "City Girl" on her Line 6 Variax electric guitar, which simulates different tunings as well as guitar types (acoustics, electrics, even 12-strings) through digital modeling. So while the strings of the solid-body Variax physically remain in standard tuning, in "City Girl" the output sounds as an acoustic in open D.

Another open-D gem from Armatrading's repertoire is "Woncha Come On Home," from *Show Some Emotion,* a haunting song about loneliness mixed with paranoia. As shown in **Example 4,** play fingerstyle, picking melodies on both the upper and lower strings. On the record, Armatrading adds a touch of African thumb piano to the guitar arrangement.

Tuning: D A D F♯ A D
Example 3 (à la "City Girl")

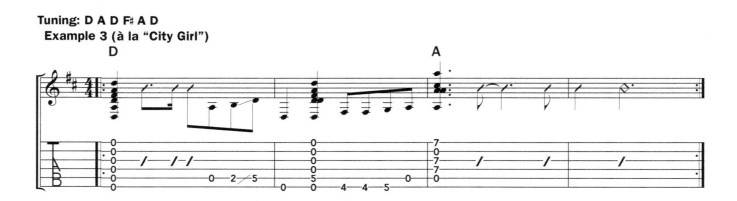

Example 4 (à la "Woncha Come On Home")

INSTRUMENTAL CHOICES

For Armatrading, the song dictates the instrumentation and arrangement, and her job is to follow. As she puts it, "The song is king or queen, whatever you want to say. The song will tell you what key it wants to be in, the tempo it wants, whether it wants to be rhythmic, whether it wants to be on the guitar and the piano. I've written songs that really, if I was sensible, I wouldn't have written it in that key, but the song says, 'This is the key that I need to be in.' So that's the key it stays in."

Within her guitar repertoire, the song also suggests the type of instrument or setup: six-string or 12-, acoustic or electric, low-tuned or standard. Songs she plays on 12-string, such as "Love and Affection," "Let It Last," and "Promise Land," wouldn't be the same on a six-string. "You need that sound, really," she says. "You need that jangly thing going."

She associates songs with specific guitars in her collection, too. On her most recent album spotlighting acoustic guitar, 2018's *Not Too Far Away,* and in concerts promoting the release, she played her Martin 00 and dreadnought guitars (see "What She Plays"), which she says have a tighter feel very different from her "laid back" Ovations.

Example 5 is based on the intro to "I Like It When We're Together," the opening track on *Not Too Far Away*, played on a low-tuned Martin. Play fingerstyle, picking the notes in each chord simultaneously with your thumb and fingers, and add a light slap with your picking fingers on beat 4. At the end of the intro, add one beat (see the change to 5/4) before resuming in 4/4 in the verse. Continuing in the song, she switches to strumming for the chorus. Her guitar arrangements often use these kinds of textural changes to create contrast from section to section.

JOAN ARMATRADING
NOT TOO FAR AWAY

Tuning: D G C F A D
Example 5 (à la "I Like It When We're Together")

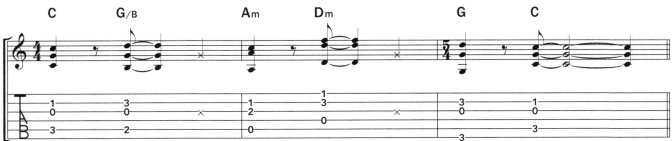

JAZZING UP THE CHORDS

Armatrading's songs tap into a much wider vocabulary than basic cowboy chords or power chords. She has a special fondness for extended chords—major and minor sevenths, ninths, 11ths, 13ths, and more—that she traces back to the early and indirect influence of her father.

"You know, my father had a guitar that he wouldn't let me play," she recalls. "The song that I heard him play was 'Blue Moon,' and it's very jazzy. So I think that's where the jazzy chords come from. He didn't show me how to play any of those chords, but I loved the sound of them."

One song that exemplifies how Armatrading uses these types of extended chords is "Kissin' and a Huggin'," from *Show Some Emotion*, which she has often cited as her favorite song to play. It's almost three songs in one, each with its own feel. Try the driving main chord riff in **Example 6a**, based on the E7#9—commonly called the Hendrix chord because of its appearance in "Purple Haze," but Armatrading's frequent use of this shape makes a strong case for calling it the Armatrading chord. At the end of the second measure, play a quick Am11 to G#7♭5 before looping back up to E7#9. The rhythm notated here is closer to recent solo performances by Armatrading than to the original recording.

Example 6a (à la "Kissin' and a Huggin'")

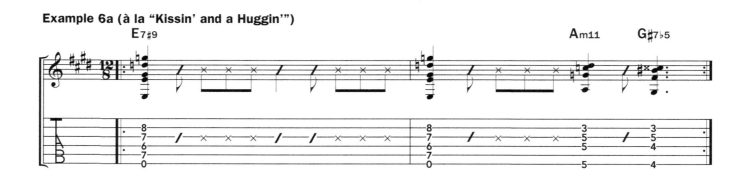

From that main riff, though, "Kissin' and a Huggin'" makes a sudden transition into a much more relaxed chorus (not shown) based on strumming straight major and minor chords. And then comes the instrumental section, which has a light jazz feel. **Example 6b** shows the chord progression: E7#9–A7–Gmaj7–Cmaj7–C13–B7♭13. The original record has electric guitar and saxophone solos; performing by herself, Armatrading solos over her own prerecorded rhythm.

Armatrading is generally conversant with the make-up of extended chords but careful not to get bogged down in theory. "I can name chords, and I try to know what it is more by the chord shape that I'm playing," she says. "But I don't really want to be playing and thinking, I am doing a ninth or a flattened 13th. I don't want to play like that. That's boring. To me, that's not musical, because music is all about feel and expression."

Interestingly, she also does not use these more sophisticated harmonies in the initial stages of songwriting. "When I'm writing, the start of the song is always a basic chord—E, F, G, D, A, B, C, that's it," she says. "You don't need anything else. Once I've written the song, then I'll start to put the advanced chords on if it needs it. If it doesn't need it, you obviously don't do it."

Example 6b

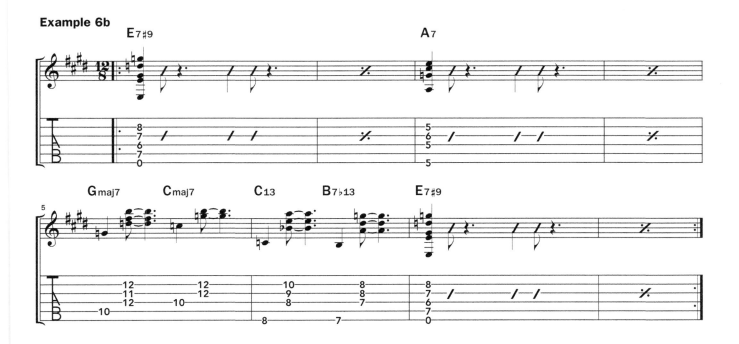

The title track from *Show Some Emotion* is another classic song that uses some jazz harmony and feel without really sounding like jazz. In the first measure of **Example 7**, play the speedy A minor pentatonic riff that carries the verses. Vintage live clips show Armatrading casually ripping through this riff—on a 12-string, no less—while singing. No easy feat.

Then the chorus of "Show Some Emotion" modulates to A major and goes into a string of minor seventh, ninth, sixth, and diminished chords, as in measures 2–9. Between the D6 and A7, play quick natural harmonics at the 12th fret on the top two strings to suggest a passing E chord. (This is a touch I noticed in live footage.)

STEPPIN' OUT

Along with her powerful rhythm, Armatrading is an adept lead player—though audiences may not always realize it. "I mean, I've been onstage with electric guitar and playing a solo," she says with a chuckle, "and the audience is looking at the other guitarist who's in the band."

Frequently, Armatrading *is* her own band. On her last six albums, going back to *Lovers Speak* in 2003, she has played nearly all the instruments (guitars, bass, keyboards, programmed drums, and so on), layering and engineering the tracks in her own studio, aka Bumpkin Studios.

Even when she's performing solo with guitar, Armatrading likes to incorporate instrumental breaks. One example is the solo version of "Steppin' Out" recorded in her *AG* video session. The song is mostly a two-chord jam, going between the I and IV (E and A shapes, tuned down a step), with a few quick touches of the V (B). She starts in open position but soon jumps up to the fifth and 12th frets for variety. And then she cuts loose in a

Standard Tuning
Example 7 (à la "Show Some Emotion")

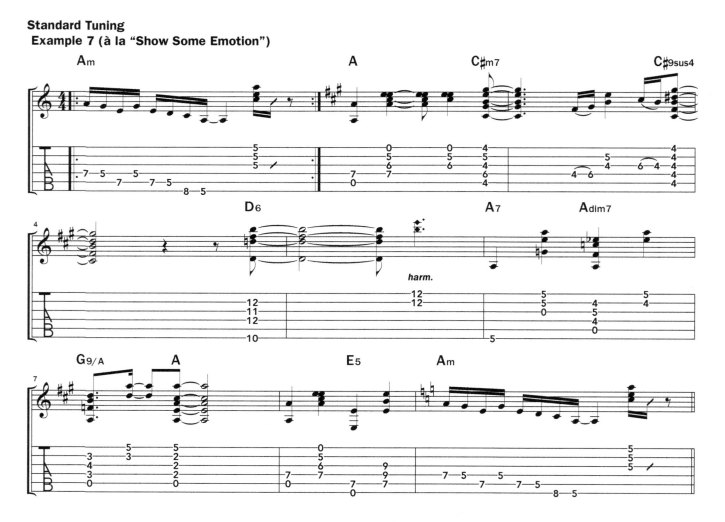

full-blown instrumental, moving around the neck and toying with the tonality with major, seventh, minor, and 7#9 voicings of E.

An excerpt from her solo is shown in **Example 8**. Start with E and A7 up at the 12th fret, and add rock-style (up and down) vibrato on the A7, which is easier with the low tuning. Then head down to the seventh and sixth frets in measure 2, followed by a single-note line in measure 3. Along the way, spice up the harmony with touches of Amaj9 (measure 2) and E7♭13#9. Throughout the solo, Armatrading plays hard, with plenty of additional percussion and open strings.

Tuning: D G C F A D
Example 8 (à la "Steppin' Out")

As you work through the example, focus more on the overall feel than on recreating every scratch and note.

"You have to naturally keep the rhythm going," she says when I ask how she approaches an improv section like this. "And when you're in the feel, then it'll happen, won't it? I'm trying not to analyze how I'm playing it or work out beforehand what the little bits will be. I just play it and hope that it works, because I can't spend my time trying to second-guess myself."

One of Armatrading's most arresting guitar moments on record is the intro to "Like Fire," from *Show Some Emotion*. In **Example 9**, again in the low tuning, open with a bluesy passage played mostly around the fifth fret. The harmony is ambiguous here, with hints of A minor and D but no obvious root chord. In measure 3, though, kick into the song's sly, funky primary groove in E, as used in the verse. Notice

how the repeating riff goes for six beats, so it starts at the beginning of measure 3, in the middle of measure 4, and again on the downbeat in measure 6.

In measures 9 and 10, slide a minor 11th shape from C♯ down to the B, and then wrap up the intro with a real stretch, a 7♯9 with a fourth-finger barre on the top two strings, climbing from A back up to B. Armatrading takes these kinds of finger-buster chord moves in stride.

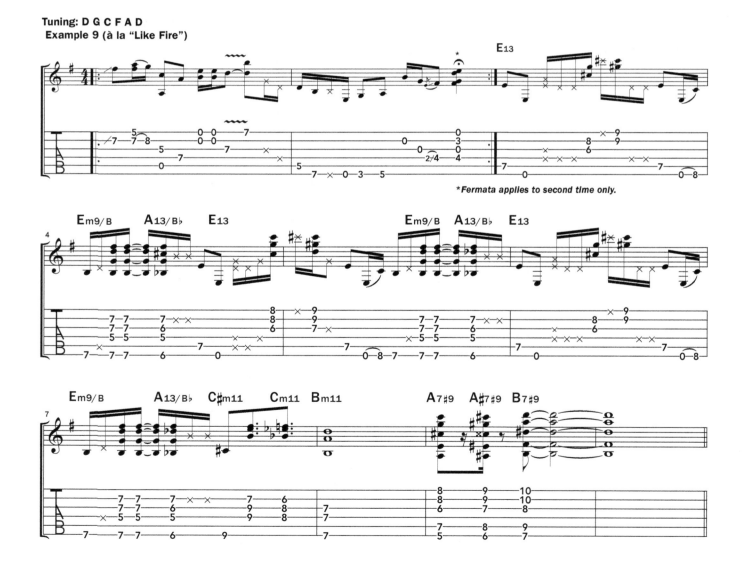

Tuning: **D G C F A D**
Example 9 (à la "Like Fire")

Fermata applies to second time only.

ON THE PATH

While Armatrading, at 71, has retired from extended touring, that doesn't mean she's hanging up her hat as a musician. Writing songs, she says, is "as natural as breathing really. I think this is what I was born to do. It's something I *have* to do, and I know I'll never stop doing it."

And for all she's accomplished over 50 years and more than 20 studio albums, she still feels the simple drive to get better on the guitar.

"I find it quite a difficult instrument to play, and I'm still learning," she reflects. "I know I'm good, but I think I could be better, so I try all the time to get better at it—just to get the chords that I want quicker and cleaner, and play better solos . . . Just understanding the guitar more. It's a lovely instrument to play, and when you get some measure of control over it, it's such a great feeling."

WHAT SHE PLAYS

Joan Armatrading has been playing Ovation guitars since the mid-1970s, and two of her current companions onstage are a six-string Custom Legend and a 12-string Legend. Among her other acoustics are two Martins, a DCPA4 cutaway dreadnought and a smaller-bodied 00-28. Live, she sometimes uses a Boss chorus pedal with her acoustics but otherwise goes direct into the mixer.

Armatrading's main electric guitar for performing is a Line 6 Variax, which uses digital modeling to create a wide range of instrument types and tunings. She runs the Variax through a Line 6 HX Stomp amp and effects processor, and has no amps onstage.

Armatrading's six- and 12-string acoustics are set up with D'Addario phosphor bronze extra-light strings (.010–.047). On electric, she uses D'Addario EXL110 nickel-wound regular lights (.010–.046). For flatpicks, she uses a .73mm Dunlop, and she's a big fan of Roadie automatic tuners for keeping her guitars and basses in tune. —*JPR*

Fingerstyle Stories

Exploring Joan Baez's Graceful and Understated Guitar Accompaniments

By Jeffrey Pepper Rodgers

This feature originally appeared in the May/June 2019 issue of Acoustic Guitar *magazine.*

In the summer of 1959, an 18-year-old singer in a bright dress strode onto the stage at the first Newport Folk Festival—a surprise guest of headliner Bob Gibson. Strumming a 12-string, Gibson kicked off the spiritual "Virgin Mary Had One Son," and she added a crystalline high harmony and sang a solo verse, her voice growing stronger line by line. On their second song, a jaunty call-and-response version of "We Are Crossing the Jordan River," she started to cut loose—her voice intense and commanding, with a nearly operatic wide vibrato. And when that song ended, in the words of singer/guitarist Dave Van Ronk (captured in David Hajdu's book *Positively Fourth Street*), "Newport absolutely exploded."

That young singer was, of course, Joan Baez, who quickly became queen of the burgeoning folk scene. After Newport, folk fans lined up around the block to hear her perform at Club 47, her home base in Cambridge, Massachusetts. In short order she was selling out concert halls around the country; her image—barefoot and cradling a guitar—graced the cover of *Time* magazine; and her first records of unadorned, centuries-old ballads and traditional songs went gold. As Bob Dylan put it in the PBS documentary *How Sweet the Sound*, "Joanie was at the forefront of a new dynamic in American music."

In the decades since, Baez has remained one of the defining artists of her generation. Understandably, the primary focus of attention on Baez's music has always been her extraordinary voice—as well as her commitment to using that voice for political causes, from the Civil Rights and antiwar movements of the 1960s up through present-day activism on issues such as immigration and climate change. There's another side of Baez's musical legacy, though, that has been a quieter but still deep influence: her guitar style. A skilled and precise fingerstyle player who helped bring parlor guitars into the spotlight, Baez modeled an approach to accompaniment that was—in keeping with her music—not flashy, but effective, elegant, and complete-sounding with no other instruments. Like her singing, Baez's guitar style is all about clarity.

This lesson takes a closer look at the guitar side of Baez, through a series of examples inspired by stand-out songs in her repertoire, from her 1960 debut to her Grammy-nominated 2018 release, *Whistle Down the Wind*. Baez, now 78, has said that album may be her last, and her concert appearances that wind up this summer will also be her farewell from touring, so it's an especially appropriate time to look back and celebrate her contributions to the landscape of the acoustic guitar.

TRADITIONAL ROOTS

Baez's introduction to the folk world came when she was teenager through a life-changing Pete Seeger concert in Palo Alto, California, where she was inspired by not only the songs but also Seeger's uncompromising political stands. She discovered great voices such as Harry Belafonte and Odetta, and when her family moved from Palo Alto to Boston in 1958, Joan and her sister Mimi (singer Mimi Fariña) found themselves right next to one of the epicenters of the folk scene—Cambridge's Harvard Square. As she noted in her 2017 induction speech at the Rock and Roll Hall of Fame, "I was lucky enough to have found my voice when coffee shops were the order of the day."

On guitar, one of Baez's formative influences was her friend Debbie Green (later the wife of singer-songwriter Eric Andersen), who taught her how to fingerpick and shared her repertoire of ballads and traditional songs. Tragic ballads like "Barbara Allen" and "Silver Dagger" became Baez's core repertoire through the early years of her career. "The ballads were unrequited love and they were beautiful, and love and death and beauty were all somehow tangled in there," Baez reflected in *How Sweet the Sound*. "Young as I was, I seemed to have a heart and soul full of the sadness that it took to be attracted to those songs, and almost only those songs. They were sad and long and beautiful. And there I was."

Example 1 is based on Baez's version of one of those songs, the Francis James Child ballad "Mary Hamilton," featured on her 1960 self-titled debut. The story is as sad as they come—Mary, a royal attendant, becomes pregnant by the king, casts her baby out to sea, and is convicted for the crime—and Baez plays and sings it with clear-eyed understatement. The guitar part follows a simple arpeggio in a style more akin to classical guitar than folk/blues fingerpicking. The example uses C shapes; to match the pitch of the original recording, tune down a half step.

Example 1 (à la "Mary Hamilton")

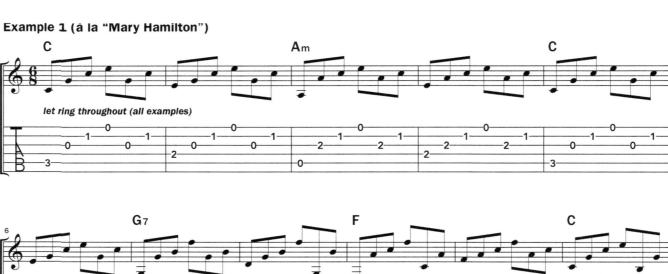

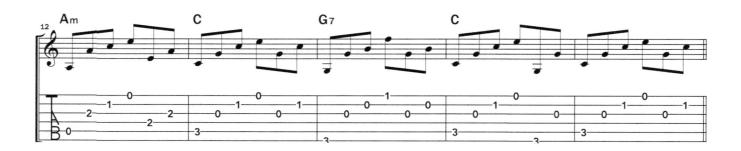

To get started, practice the picking pattern just on the C in the first two measures. Finger/string assignments can be flexible, but as a rule, pick the bottom three strings with your thumb, the third string with your index, second string with the middle, and first string with the ring. Baez typically plays with a plastic thumbpick and three fingerpicks (she uses Alaska Piks—more on that later), but bare fingers work fine, too.

Another traditional song from her debut album, "House of the Rising Sun" is the basis of **Example 2**. The example is shown in the key of E minor, but again, on the original recording the guitar is tuned down—in this case, down a whole step to D. So tune accordingly if you want to play along with Baez's track.

"House of the Rising Sun" has many variations, and you'll note that the progression here differs from the Animals' 1964 version that became the de facto standard. As in Ex. 1, you are picking arpeggios but also adding some partial chords. For the double-stops on the treble strings (as on beat 2 of the first two measures), pick the strings simultaneously with your fingers. When you're playing two or three notes together in the bass (as on the first beat of bar 5), strum with your thumb. In measures 3, 5, and 7, play eighth-note triplets to add rhythmic variety.

Example 2 (à la "House of the Rising Sun")

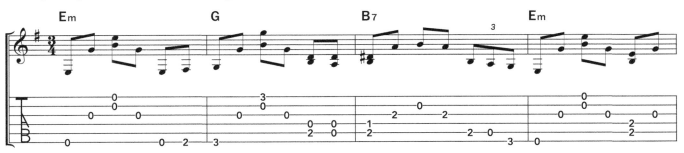

Example 3 shows a fingerpicking pattern used in the spiritual "Oh Freedom," which Baez sang at the 1963 March on Washington. The 1960 recording by Harry Belafonte, one of Baez's early inspirations, is all vocal, and Baez sings it a cappella, too, on the Live at Newport compilation of her festival performances from 1963–65. A live version of "Oh Freedom" with guitar can be heard on the soundtrack to *How Sweet the Sound*. The picking style in this example is similar to what's used in Ex. 1, except that the arpeggio is more linear—it goes up to

the first string and then back down. Mark Goldenberg, who played nylon-string guitar on Baez's latest album, notes that these types of patterns give Baez's playing a "fluid rolling quality." Throughout, let strings ring as much as possible, for a legato sound.

It's worth noting that the 12-fret parlor guitars that Baez favors—in particular petite 0- and 00-size Martin models—are ideal for this type of playing, with their easy articulation, balanced sound, and fingerstyle-friendly string spacing (see "Joan Baez's Martin Guitars" p. 31).

Example 3 (à la "Oh Freedom")

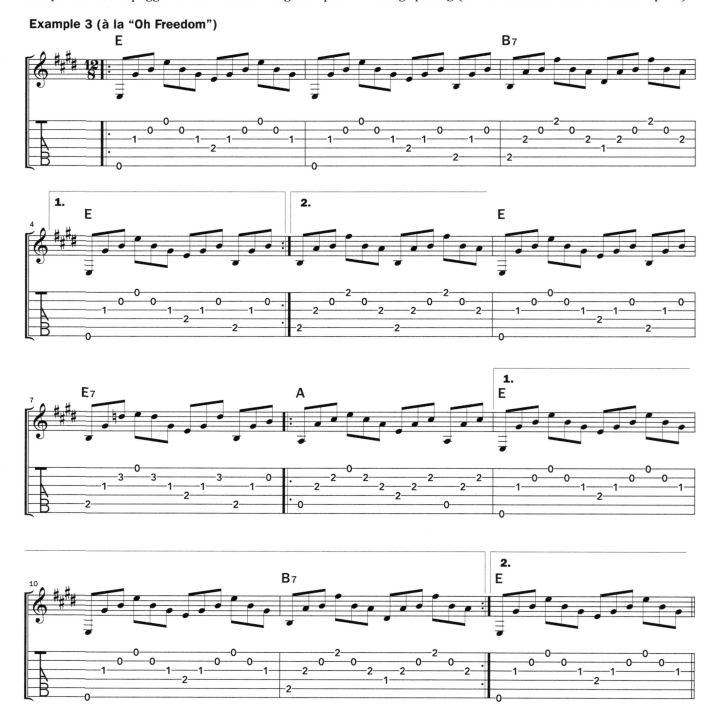

THUMB AND STRUM

Not all of Baez's early songs were slow ballads. "The Lily of the West," a traditional Irish song featured on her second album, *Vol. 2*, in 1961, is a bit of a picking workout. The guitar part is more like flatpicking accompaniment, or Carter-style picking, with bass notes followed by brush strums on the high strings. Try it in **Example 4**. Use E-minor shapes and capo up at the sixth fret to sound in Bb minor.

The opening measures lay out the basic pattern: bass note on beat 1, one or two strums on 2, hammer-on for the bass note on 3, and one or two strums on 4. Use your thumb for the bass notes, and strum up or down with your fingers. If you prefer fingerpicks, this is where the type of picks matters. Fingerpicks that curve over the pad of your fingers will catch on the strings if you try to strum down (toward the first string). The Alaska Piks Baez uses fit over your nail—they are basically a reinforcement

or extension of your nail—so they allow you to pick both up and down, as with banjo frailing. Where the notation shows eighth notes on *Vol. 2*, 1961 the treble strings, try a down-up strum with your index alone or index and middle fingers together. The motion is more like a light flick than a hard strum.

Baez's original recording zips along at about 144 bpm, which will keep your picking hand busy. To learn this song, "slow it way down," advises Allison Shapira, who covers the Baez repertoire in the tribute duo Joan and Joni along with fellow songwriter Kipyn Martin. "Build up muscle memory so both the picking pattern and the hammers become second nature, and then slowly speed it up."

In measures 5–12, create a dramatic intro by replacing the bass notes with a melodic line that descends from the fourth fret of the third string all the way down to the open sixth string, while keeping the strums going on beats 2 and 4.

Example 4 (à la "The Lily of the West")
Capo VI

THE DYLAN CONNECTION

In addition to popularizing many traditional songs, Baez has been influential for spotlighting the work of contemporary songwriters—most famously, the early music of Bob Dylan. She first heard the little-known troubadour in 1961 at Gerde's Folk City in New York's Greenwich Village—she later described him a "scruffy little mess" at the time, but she found him captivating nonetheless. Two years later Baez and Dylan played a couple of duets at Newport and she invited him on tour, using her star power to introduce him to mainstream audiences. The two musicians were romantically involved for a while, too, but their musical and personal relationship soon frayed, as captured in painful detail in *Don't Look Back*, the documentary chronicling Dylan's 1965 tour of England.

Baez has recorded a slew of Dylan songs, including a full album's worth on *Any Day Now* in 1968. One of her notable Dylan covers is "Forever Young," which she put out as a single in 1974, shortly after Dylan himself released it on *Planet Waves*. Baez played an accompaniment part similar to **Example 5**. Capo at the second fret to sound in the key of A. In the first four bars, move up the neck on the second and fourth strings before settling into the picking pattern on the G shape. The quick hammer-on/pull-off in bar 5 recurs at the end of the example, to punctuate the end of a verse.

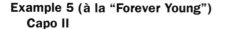

Example 5 (à la "Forever Young")
Capo II

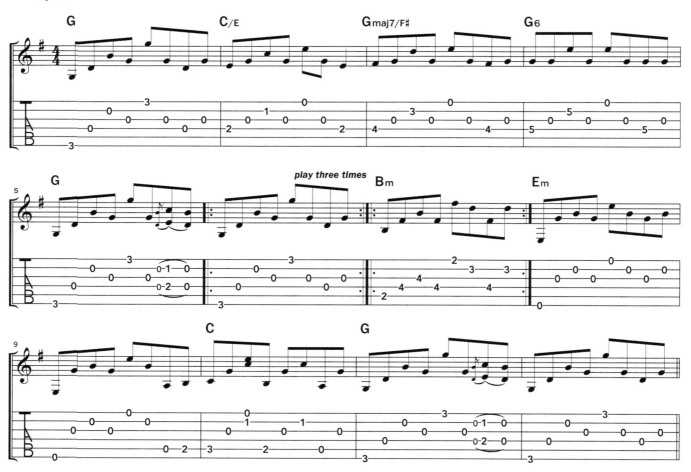

Example 6 (à la "Diamonds and Rust")

Dylan also inspired some of Baez's own songwriting. In "To Bobby," released in 1972, she made a direct (and, she understood later, futile) appeal to Dylan to pick up the mantle of political protest. And a few years later, a phone call from Dylan stirred one of her best original songs, "Diamonds and Rust"—memorably turned into a hard-rocking anthem by Judas Priest. **Example 6** shows a passage similar to Baez's intro in that haunting song.

In "Diamonds and Rust," the Spanish flavor of Baez's guitar style shows through, especially in the recurring fingerstyle rolls, as in measure 2, starting right after the downbeat. Pick the top three strings with your index, middle, and ring fingers in quick succession, aiming for a smooth and even flow of notes. Starting in measure 4, the low notes of the pattern climb up the fourth and third strings—this is reminiscent of the intro passage in Ex. 4, except ascending rather than descending.

TELLING THE STORY

The final example of this lesson is inspired by the title track of Baez's most recent album, *Whistle Down the Wind*. Though her voice has lost some of its range and power, Baez's singing on the album is emotive and deeply affecting, and her playing is featured on most of the tracks—she brought out her original 1929 0-45 for the sessions. Producer Joe Henry, as in many of his projects, wanted to take a live, organic approach. The sessions started with all the players listening to Baez play and sing the songs alone, recalls Mark Goldenberg.

"Originally Joe had me there to support Joan in the event that she had difficulty playing her parts as she sang," says Goldenberg. "But that did not turn out to be the case, so I moved over to nylon-string. Greg Leisz was on electric, steel, mandolin, and everything else. It was then a matter of finding parts that would fit in the overall picture. We had a full band playing live, with Joe gently coaxing the best out of everyone. Those were great sessions."

On "Whistle Down the Wind," one of two Tom Waits songs on the album, the rich tones of Baez's guitar are at the center of the arrangement. **Example 7** shows a part similar to her intro. Use key-of-A shapes (and capo at the first fret to be in the album key), and add hammer-ons, pull-offs, and slides as shown to bring out a bit of melody on the second string. In several spots, use chord rolls (indicated with wavy vertical lines); these are similar to the rolls used in Ex. 6, except played faster, so the sound registers as a chord rather than a quick series of single notes. You could play these chord rolls as a strum with your finger(s), slowed down enough that the notes register individually, but you can get a cleaner sound by picking each string in succession.

As you delve into these examples, remember that the guitar parts don't exist in isolation—they are carefully crafted to support the song's melody and mood. "The dynamics of her playing are coupled to the dynamics of her singing," notes Scott Nygaard, the flatpicker (and former *AG* editor) who has performed with Baez's band. Pay attention, he says, to "how she uses both to communicate the feeling and meaning of the song she's singing."

That is, to me, the most important lesson of Baez's guitar style. Good technique is necessary to create accompaniment parts that are clear, graceful, and tonally rich, but ultimately the melody and the words matter most. The job of the guitar is to help tell the story. **AG**

Example 7 (à la "Whistle Down the Wind")
Capo I

JOAN BAEZ'S MARTIN GUITARS

Joan Baez found her soulmate guitar, a 1929 Martin 0-45, for a few hundred dollars in the early '60s. "It was my first serious folk guitar," Baez recalled in a PBS *Craft in America* documentary about C. F. Martin & Co. "I had a Goya with gut strings, then I had a gigantic Gibson which hung around my knees, and I've never been able to deal with a really large guitar at all." Cradling her 0-45, she added, "So this one just became home."

Baez's main touring guitars are two Martin 0-45JBs, the limited-edition models that commemorate her original 0-45. When Martin took apart that 0-45 in the 1990s in order to study it, they discovered that a luthier who'd worked on the guitar years before left some hidden commentary inside: "Too bad you're a Communist!" So the remakes include that handwritten inscription, too, which can be seen with an inspection mirror. Other Martin parlor guitars that Baez played in her early years include a 00-45 and a circa 1880 0-40. Martin acquired the 0-40 in 2015 and added the instrument to the collection at the Martin Guitar Museum.

PHOTO COURTESY OF C.F. MARTIN & CO.

Band in a Box

An Exclusive Lesson with Legendary Songwriter and Fingerstyle Guitar Master Bruce Cockburn

By Jeffrey Pepper Rodgers

O ver a career spanning five decades, Bruce Cockburn has traversed an extraordinarily wide landscape on the guitar, from fingerstyle folk, country blues, and gospel to edgy rock and exploratory jazz—all in the service of his songwriting muse. What's even more remarkable is that he's done all this not just as a bandleader but also as a solo acoustic performer. In Cockburn's hands, the guitar becomes a true band in a box, delivering powerful grooves, riffs, melodies, harmonized lines, and improvised solos in real time.

And at 74, Cockburn is certainly not done exploring the instrument, as is obvious from a spin of *Crowing Ignites*, his 34th album and first-ever collection of all new instrumentals (2005's *Speechless* compiled previously released instrumentals along with a few new tracks). The title *Crowing Ignites* is a rough translation of "Accendit Cantu," which adorns the old Cockburn family crest. As does so much of his music, the album ranges across folk, blues, jazz, and shades in between, with virtuosic playing primarily on six-string, 12-string, and baritone acoustics.

Getting a handle on Cockburn's multilayered guitar style isn't easy, even for Cockburn himself. "I don't think about how I do it—I just do it," he says on the phone from his home in San Francisco. "But it's actually quite interesting to try and make it into something communicable." That is exactly what Cockburn accomplishes in this lesson: He breaks down the key components of his style and demonstrates them through a series of examples drawn from his songs.

Below, you can learn the core guitar parts from some of Cockburn's best-known songs, such as "Wondering Where the Lions Are" and "Pacing the Cage," as well as other gems from across his career. The result is perhaps the closest and clearest view ever of this guitar master at work.

THE ALTERNATING BASS

In Cockburn's view, the logical way to break down his approach to guitar is not by style or genre—he's always been dedicated to crossing stylistic boundaries anyway—but by picking-hand technique. Though the

This feature originally appeared in the September/October 2019 issue of Acoustic Guitar *magazine.*

details and feel vary, most of his songs can be boiled down to a few right-hand fingerstyle techniques—one of which is the classic alternating bass style, as he learned especially from his early woodshedding with the music of Mississippi John Hurt. In a video for *AG*'s Sessions series, Cockburn in fact began with a verse of Hurt's "My Creole Belle," in which the fingers double the vocal melody over the alternating bass—an idea that he has employed in many songs over the years.

In a similar vein, **Example 1** comes from literally the beginning of Cockburn's recording career: "Going to the Country," track one on his self-titled 1970 debut. He plays in standard tuning out of G shapes, with his thumb holding down the sixth string at the third fret (more below on his extensive use of the thumb for fretting). The example shows the intro, where he picks a melodic line on the top two strings that harmonizes with the vocal. During the verses, his guitar doubles the vocal melody.

Before taping this session, Cockburn hadn't played this song in many years and pointed out that he can't fully reproduce the original recording, on which he used fingerpicks—an approach he soon abandoned. "When I first started using picks I liked the tone," he recalls. "But I soon discovered that with fingerpicks on, you can't really do downstrokes with your fingers, because the fingerpicks go flying into the audience's drink."

Playing with bare fingers, as Cockburn has done ever since those earliest days, gives the flexibility to combine upstrokes and downstrokes, picking, and strumming. Bare fingers also help create the kind of warm, round tone that was characteristic of Hurt's music.

Example 1 (à la "Going to the Country")

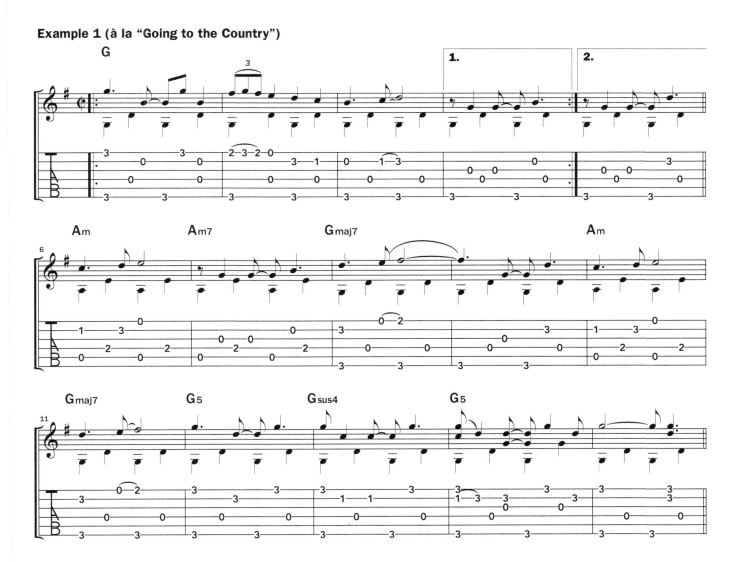

Perhaps even more in the Mississippi John Hurt style is "Pacing the Cage," a luminous ballad from Cockburn's 1996 album *The Charity of Night*. In **Example 2**, capo at the fourth fret and use C shapes—as Hurt himself often did. In the song's main pattern, alternate the bass between the fifth and fourth strings as the chords move from C to G/B to Fsus2/A. On the treble side, pick double-stops on the first and second strings for the C and G/B, and then add in the third string on the Fsus2/A. In measure 2, Cockburn uses a fourth-finger barre on top of the G/B chord, but you may find it easier (as I do) to use the third and fourth fingers together on those top strings instead.

The alternating bass is also at the root of "Wondering Where the Lions Are," from his 1979 breakthrough album, *Dancing in the Dragon's Jaws*. With its infectious reggae-like groove (delivered in the studio with the help of a Jamaican rhythm section), "Lions" became a Top 40 hit in the US. Drop your sixth string to D, capo at the second fret, and try the main rhythm pattern in **Example 3**. For much of the song, your fretting hand stays five frets above the capo.

Again, you need your thumb for fretting the G shape. "When I was first taking lessons eons ago, I was taught that it was a terrible thing to fret with your thumb," Cockburn says. "But then I saw some great old blues guys doing it, and I thought, that doesn't sound so terrible to me. So it just became part of my toolkit, and it eventually became an indispensable part."

Example 2 (à la "Pacing the Cage")
Capo IV

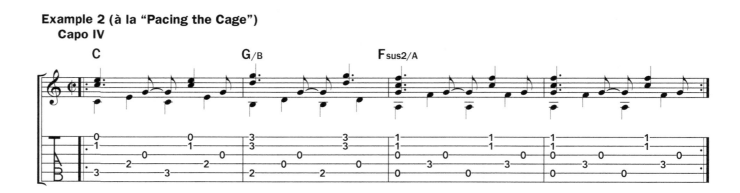

Example 3 (à la "Wondering Where the Lions Are")
Tuning: D A D G B E, Capo II

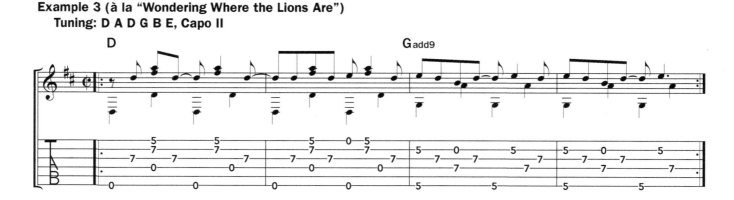

THE DRONE BASS

The other main picking-hand technique in Cockburn's music is the monotone or drone bass, as heard particularly in blues—in which the thumb plays a rhythmic pulse on a single string, often with palm muting for a more percussive effect.

At times Cockburn does use the drone bass in a straight-up blues context. *Crowing Ignites* has two great examples. In "The Groan," he plays a steady bass on the fifth string, with a 12/8 blues shuffle feel, using what he refers to as Gsus tuning (D G D G C D). And in "Blind Willie," a blues in A (for which he tunes the second string down to A), he plays a quarter-note pulse on the open fifth string for the entire song. **Example 4**, from "Blind Willie," shows a sample of the kind of riffing that you can do up and down the neck over the open-string bass.

The basic idea of playing over a drone bass, though, can apply far beyond blues, Cockburn notes. "Way back in the day when I was 'studying' jazz at Berklee—I'm putting the studying in quotes because I wasn't a very good student—I discovered that I really didn't like chords that much," he says. "I don't feel exactly like this now, but I was much more drawn to Asian music of various kinds that doesn't use Western harmonies, where the intervals that you might think of in a harmonic way are measured against a droning bass rather than against each other as they move around. So a lot of what I do is informed by a desire to make use of that phenomenon."

Example 4 (à la "Blind Willie")
Tuning: E A D G A E

The new song "Bardo Rush" runs with this idea. Tuned to D modal or double dropped D (first and sixth strings to D), Cockburn plays a monotone bass on the sixth string for the entire song, adding all sorts of chord melody and jazzy riffs on top. Try an excerpt in **Example 5**. Play the harmonized melody with your fingers over the driving bass drone.

In learning any of Cockburn's songs, whether with an alternating bass or a drone bass, the bass line is the best place to start. Practice the thumb until its movement is automatic, then work on adding the treble side.

Example 5 (à la "Bardo Rush")
Tuning: D A D G B D

DRONE BASS WITH CHORDS

Cockburn also uses the drone bass technique in songs that do change chords. A famous example is "If I Had a Rocket Launcher," written in response to Cockburn's visit to a Guatemalan refugee camp in Mexico in the early '80s. As you can see in the full transcription of his *AG* studio performance in the September/October 2019 issue of *AG*, Cockburn keeps a steady bass going throughout. In the instrumental section, he employs his thumb to fret the bass note under the C so he can continue to solo with his other fingers.

In the videos you'll notice that Cockburn often anchors his right-hand pinky on the pickguard—either keeping it planted or dropping onto the top when he digs in a little harder. This support, he finds, is essential for creating the kind of rhythmic momentum he's looking for. "When you want to bear down on a bass rhythm, you kind of need [the anchor], whether it's an alternating bass or a single-note bass," he says. "I need that anchor to really crunch into it."

Another song that uses a drone bass under changing chords is "Last Night of the World," originally released in 1999 on *Breakfast in New Orleans, Dinner in Timbuktu*. That track featured full-band backing, but as you can hear in the solo version on *Slice O Life*, the guitar part sounds complete on its own. In **Example 6**, drop your third string a half step to F♯, and leave all the others at their standard pitches, for the signature tuning Cockburn calls drop F (see "A Cockburn Tuning Sampler"). Capo at the third fret. Thump out a rock rhythm with your thumb, staying on the open sixth string until the last phrase of each verse. The example shows the riff that serves as the intro and continues under much of the verse. As in so many of Cockburn's songs, your fingers create a little melodic motif on top of the bass.

Example 6 (à la "Last Night of the World")
Tuning: E A D F♯ B E, Capo III

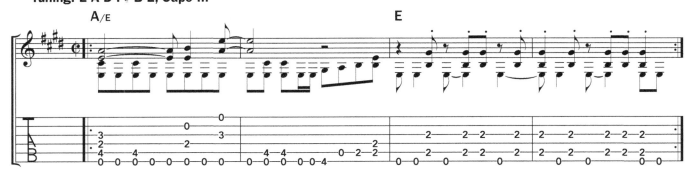

MIXING IT UP

The last two songs in this lesson use a mixture of picking approaches. "After the Rain," also played in drop-F tuning, comes from *Dancing in the Dragon's Jaws*, and is a great example of Cockburn's fusion of acoustic folk and jazz. Much of **Example 7** uses a drone bass, with single-note melodies and jazz-flavored chords on top. There's also a popping fingerstyle rhythm that Cockburn often uses, where you play quick, staccato bass notes and chords with a percussive slap on the backbeats, as in measures 7–8. At the end the chorus, there's a bit of strumming—a rarity in Cockburn's music. He is much more apt to pick multiple strings simultaneously than strum across them.

As an interesting aside, the inspiration for "After the Rain" came from an unexpected source: the Bee Gees. The song, says Cockburn, is "a very loose acoustic translation of the groove of 'Stayin' Alive.'"

Example 7 (à la "After the Rain")
Tuning: E A D F♯ B E

*S = percussive slap with picking hand

The final examples come from "Lovers in a Dangerous Time," which kicked off the 1984 album *Stealing Fire*—a period in which Cockburn's songwriting became more politically charged and, not coincidentally, more electric and band-oriented, too. Cockburn played electric guitar on the original track with a full band, strumming power chord shapes. That sound works with a band but would be boring in a solo context, Cockburn feels. So instead, he uses the rolling picking pattern in **Example 8**, which bears some similarities to his part in "After the Rain." In the instrumental section, as shown in **Example 9**, pick pairs of strings with your thumb as you play fretted notes up the neck alongside open treble strings.

These examples are, of course, a tiny sampling of the music that Cockburn has created over the last 50 years. But the fingerstyle techniques at work here can be heard across his vast catalog, applied to various types of grooves, chord progressions, and melodies. As Cockburn puts it at the close of the video, "Other songs have different details, but the basic styles tend to rotate around that axis."

Beyond covering Cockburn's work, you can also apply aspects of his style to your own songs and arrangements. Rather than using thick chords, try reducing your guitar parts—start by establishing a bass line, and then add single notes and partial chords on top. Focus on the groove, which really starts with the bass. Use tunings and capo positions that give you open-string bass notes, and therefore freedom to travel around the neck. And try doubling or harmonizing with the vocal melody on the guitar. The key is to think of the guitar as a multi-voiced instrument—rhythm section, backup singer, and soloist all at once.

Example 8 (à la "Lovers in a Dangerous Time")

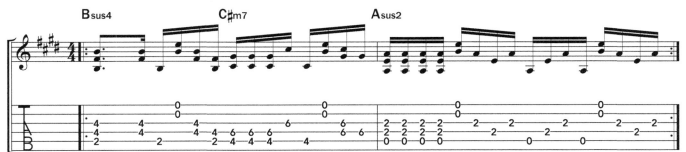

Example 9 (à la "Lovers in a Dangerous Time")

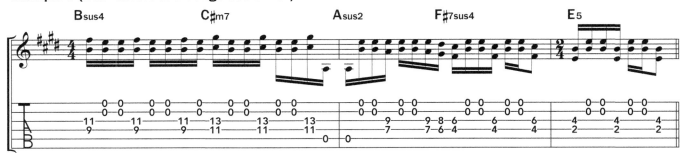

A COCKBURN TUNING SAMPLER

In his early days, Cockburn was leery of relying on alternate tunings to generate new sounds. "My beef with open tunings back in the '60s, when everybody was using them, was that people really didn't learn their instrument," he says. "They learned four or five fingerings, and then they just changed the tuning and thought they were doing something different. But it was a boring way to play guitar, and a boring thing to listen to."

As you can see in the list at right, Cockburn has recorded some songs in open-chord tunings, like open D and, more often, open C. Further off the beaten track is his open Dm7 tuning, D A C G C F, and a variation with F on the bottom, F A C G C F, that gives you an Fadd9 chord. On the new blues "The Groan," he uses D G D G C D—an open Gsus4 with a fourth (C) replacing the third (B), a similar concept to DADGAD (where you replace the third, F#, in open D tuning with the fourth, G).

For the most part, though, he is inclined to stay fairly close to standard tuning, or retune just one or two strings, as with dropped D (sixth string to D), D modal (first and sixth strings to D), and the tuning he calls drop F#, with only the third string tuned down to F#.

In another interesting tuning used on *Crowing Ignites*, he drops only the second string to A. If you also drop the first string to D, you get the tuning Cockburn calls EGAD—E A D G A D—which facilitates jazz pianoesque harmonies. "It's very McCoy Tyner–like," he says. "You get all these fourths that are just right there, easy to get to."

OPEN-CHORD TUNINGS

Open D (D A D F# A D): "Sunwheel Dance" (capo 2)

Open C (C G C G C E): "Foxglove" (capo 1), "Soul of a Man," "Easter"

Open Dm7 (D A C G C F): "Wait No More" (capo 3), "Down to the Delta," "Live On My Mind"

Fadd9 (F A C G C F): "Dust and Diesel"

Gsus4 (D G D G C D): "The Groan"

RETUNING ONE OR TWO STRINGS FROM STANDARD

Dropped D (D A D G B E): "Call It Democracy," "Wondering Where the Lions Are" (capo 2), "If a Tree Falls," "Mystery," "How I Spent My Fall Vacation" (capo 2 on original recording, no capo on Slice o Life)

D modal (D A D G B D): "Use Me While You Can," "Bardo Rush"

Drop F# (E A D F# B E): "After the Rain," "Last Night of the World" (capo 3), "Fascist Architecture," "Don't Feel Your Touch," "Mango" (capo 1), "World of Wonders" (solo version on *Slice O Life*, with capo 5)

E A D G A E "Blind Willie"

E A D G A D (aka EGAD): "Bone on Bone," "Strange Waters," "Jerusalem Poker," "The Iris of the World"

WHAT BRUCE COCKBURN PLAYS

Cockburn's mainstay acoustics are built by Toronto luthier Linda Manzer. Live, he plays his six- and 12-string Manzers, plus a metal-bodied Dobro (pictured here). On much of *Crowing Ignites*, he played a Boucher Studio Goose OM hybrid model, with Canadian maple back and sides, that was given to him during his 2017 induction into the Canadian Songwriters Hall of Fame alongside Neil Young and others. Also heard on the album is a Karol baritone acoustic.

For amplification, the Manzers have Fishman undersaddle pickups and Audio-Technica internal mics, with separate outputs. The mics run directly to the PA, while the pickups go through a chain with a Boss tuner, Moog tremolo, two Boss echo pedals, and TC Electronic reverb and chorus. "A stereo signal then goes to the PA," says Cockburn, "so altogether there are three guitar channels." The Dobro has a similar dual-source setup, with a Telecaster pickup and a custom internal mic.

He typically sets up his acoustics with light-gauge Martin Marquis 80/20 bronze strings, and he uses Shubb and Kyser capos.

WIKIMEDIA PHOTO, VIA ABC AND AN EVENING WITH JOHN DENVER.

This Old Guitar

John Denver and His Elegant Fretwork

By Jeffrey Pepper Rodgers

In the 1970s, the music of John Denver seemed to be everywhere. Denver scored seven Top 10 singles within a few years, from "Take Me Home, Country Roads" in 1971 to "I'm Sorry" in '75. His albums and songs crossed over the pop, country, and easy listening charts and found multigenerational fans around the world. With his wirerimmed glasses, honeyed voice, and chiming flattop guitar, Denver serenaded audiences on his own TV specials and sang with everyone from the Carpenters to Frank Sinatra to the Muppets.

How did such a gentle and sincere troubadour, straight out of the folk coffeehouse circuit, become a global superstar? Denver himself put his finger on one reason. "For a long time now it hasn't been OK to acknowledge certain things about yourself," he told *The New York Times* in 1976. "For example, that you love your old lady. That it feels

This feature originally appeared in the March/April 2020 issue of Acoustic Guitar *magazine.*

good to be out in the sunshine. That every once in a while on a rainy day you feel sad. That life is good. As I have been able to communicate those things for myself and to reach a large audience, that gives them support in feeling those things... Nobody else is singing these songs. Everybody else is talking about how hard life is, and here I am singing about how good it is to be alive."

In the '80s and beyond, the pop-music spotlight on Denver dimmed with the inevitable shifts in musical and cultural fashions, but he continued singing about love, nature, and gratitude until his life was cut short in the crash of an experimental plane he was flying in 1997. And thanks to his gift for simple and emotionally direct expression, the songs Denver wrote and interpreted have remained standard repertoire for any musicians who sing with an acoustic guitar—even if they haven't always wanted to broadcast that fact.

"I grew up listening to a lot of music, but no small part was taken up by John Denver's music," Dave Matthews said in an *NPR* interview after he contributed a version of Denver's "Take Me to Tomorrow" to the 2013 tribute album *The Music Is You*. "I think he was a staple for a lot of people. In a way, he was sort of mocked by the industry that he was at the top of, and mocked by what was considered cool. So there was even a time when maybe I was a little embarrassed that I had an affection for him, and maybe hid it when I was trying my best to be cool."

While Denver's graceful melodies and mellifluous voice took center stage in his music, a central feature of all his songs was his crisp guitar work, primarily fingerstyle on both six- and 12-string guitars. He wasn't a showy player but took great care to craft guitar parts that subtly supported the vocal, often adding melodic riffs and embellishments that became inseparable from his songs. This lesson takes a tour through Denver's guitar style by way of examples inspired by some of his most enduring songs.

FIRST LOVE

The guitar that got John Denver—born Henry John Deutschendorf—started on the music path came to him from his grandmother when he was 11 years old. That instrument was a Gibson L-37 archtop from around the late '30s (though Denver himself often said it was built in 1910). On that Gibson, Denver learned to play songs from the Everly Brothers and other hitmakers of the 1950s, and by the early '60s he was hooked by the Kingston Trio and leading voices of the folk revival like Joan Baez, Tom Paxton, the New Christy Minstrels, the Chad Mitchell Trio, and Peter, Paul, and Mary. After Chad Mitchell left his namesake trio in 1965, Denver got his first big break as a member of the group, which continued to tour as the Mitchell Trio through the late '60s.

Denver's L-37, which currently resides at the Musical Instrument Museum in Phoenix, Arizona, went through some misadventures. At a July Fourth party one summer when Denver was working at a lumber camp in Washington state, a member of the rowdy crew apparently objected to Denver playing a Hank Williams song and bashed him with the guitar—an event memorialized with a crack across its top. Later, the Gibson went missing for about four years, and Denver celebrated its return in the song "This Old Guitar," released on the

multi-platinum album *Back Home Again*. In concert, he performed the song solo, spotlighting his connection with the instrument that, as the lyrics go, "gave me my life, my living."

"I can't really tell you how thrilled I was about getting it back," he said when introducing his Gibson, and the song he wrote about it, in a 1974 TV special. "I couldn't wait to get back to the hotel where I was staying at here in Los Angeles, and just sit down and be with the guitar again and play it. I did that. I got back to the hotel and we got very comfortable. I told it all that had happened to me since the last time I'd seen it. It told me a few stories. But somewhere in the conversation, we found this song."

"This Old Guitar" is a classic folk ballad, fingerpicked with C shapes and a pattern similar to **Example 1**. Capo at the second fret to play in Denver's key of D major. Keep a steady alternating bass going throughout—pick all the notes notated with down stems with your thumb. Denver normally played with a thumbpick and fingerpicks, but bare fingers (as I use on the accompanying videos) also work fine, producing a softer and rounder sound.

The basic shapes are shown in the chord grids, but notice how at the ends of measures you often change

Example 1 (à la "This Old Guitar")
Capo II

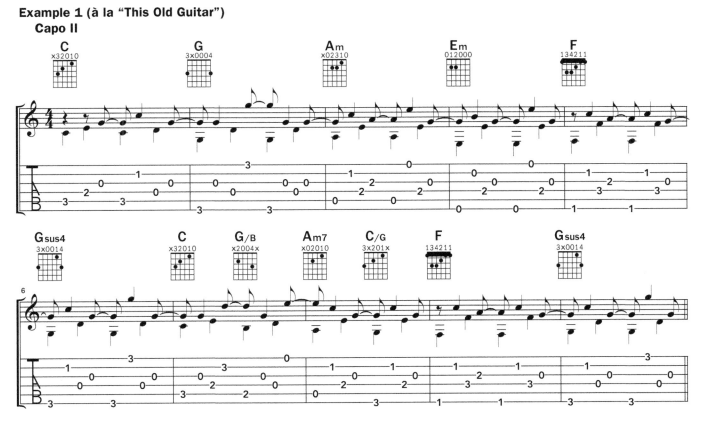

a note to anticipate the next chord. In measure 3, on the "and" of beat 4, for instance, play the third string open to lead to the E minor chord. In measure 7, both the D on the second string and E on the first string function similarly, anticipating the next chord and creating a little syncopated melody.

TAKING FLIGHT

Denver first made his mark as a songwriter with "Leaving on a Jet Plane." In his autobiography, *Take Me Home*, Denver described the song's birth one night in Virginia. "I picked up my guitar and wrote a song with my soul wide open and my mind picturing the scene as it stood before me, real enough to touch," he wrote. "I called it 'Oh, Babe, I Hate to Go.' I wrote the song not so much out of the experience of feeling that way for someone, as out of the longing to have someone to love."

In 1966, Denver included the song on his self-released record *John Denver Sings*—it was the album's sole original alongside four Beatles songs and other covers—and pressed a few hundred copies to give as Christmas gifts. One disc wound up in the hands of Peter, Paul, and Mary, who released their version of the song (which Denver had retitled as "Leaving on a Jet Plane" at the urging of producer Milt Okun) in 1967 on *Album 1700*. Two years later, "Leaving on a Jet Plane" had taken on new associations as a Vietnam War song; Peter, Paul, and Mary's cover was released as a single and became a No. 1 hit.

Though Peter, Paul, and Mary dressed up "Jet Plane" with some major sevenths and chord substitutions, Denver's rendition used a dead simple I–IV–V progression in G. In fact, as former Denver lead player Pete Huttlinger noted in his four-volume set of Homespun videos teaching Denver's songs, Denver stripped down the chord/bass movement in "Jet Plane" even further late in his career: He played the C as a C/G (in other words, keeping the same bass note under both the G and C chords) until the final chorus.

Denver picked "Jet Plane" on a 12-string. On six-string, the sound is less sparkly but still effective. The first four measures of **Example 2** are based on his intro, which hangs on the V chord (D). Over a drone bass on the open fourth string, play a melodic riff

Example 2 (à la "Leaving on a Jet Plane")

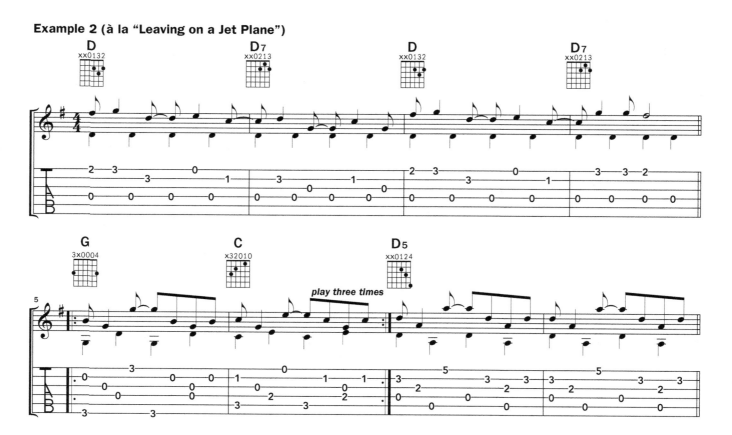

on the top strings, mostly on the offbeats. During the verse, shift between G and C (as in measures 5 and 6) three times and then move to a D5 (with your fourth finger on string 1, fret 5).

ALMOST HEAVEN

The song that really launched Denver as a solo artist was "Take Me Home, Country Roads," first released on the 1971 album *Poems, Prayers, and Promises* and co-written with Bill Danoff and Taffy Nivert. The duo, who performed at the time as Fat City, was also the source of "I Guess He'd Rather Be in Colorado" (which, though seemingly tailor-made for Denver, was actually written about banjo picker and author Dick Weissman) and other staples of Denver's repertoire.

During a late-night hang after a show at the Cellar Door in Washington, D.C., Danoff and Nivert shared with Denver a fledgling version of "Country Roads." Danoff thought the song would be a good fit for Johnny Cash and didn't expect Denver to like it, but Denver was immediately smitten and helped Danoff and Nivert finish the song in the wee hours. They performed it the following night and recorded it together for Denver's album a few months later.

Though many players strum "Country Roads" (and sometimes Denver himself did), it was normally a fingerpicking tune. In **Example 3**, run an alternating bass on three strings: On the A, for instance, play strings 5, 4, 6, 4. Over the D chord in measure 7, pause the alternation for a moment to play a descending bass line back to the A. One somewhat tricky maneuver comes in measure 2, where you hammer on to the second-string D at the same time you pick the low E bass note.

Example 3 (à la "Take Me Home, Country Roads")

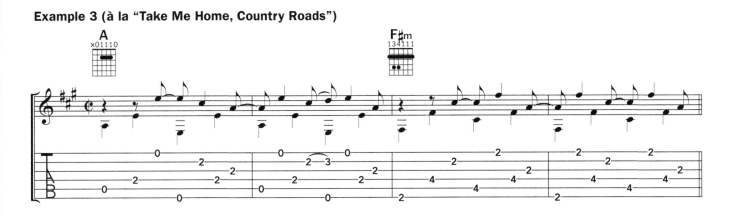

Example 4 tips its hat to the lead playing of Denver side-man Mike Taylor. The riffs shown fit over the "Country Roads" chorus progression and decorate the chords with double-stops and arpeggios. If you want to play the example with a flatpick, use hybrid picking for measures 1 and 7: Play the lower note with the pick and the upper note with your middle finger.

In addition to playing lead guitar, Mike Taylor, who passed away in 2010, was Denver's co-writer on "Rocky Mountain High," as well as another hit from *Poems, Prayers, and Promises*, "Sunshine on My Shoulders." In his autobiography, Denver recalled writing the latter song "in a fit of melancholy one wet and dismal late-winter/early-spring day in Minnesota—the kind of day that makes every Minnesotan think about going down to Mexico."

Example 4 (à la "Take Me Home, Country Roads")

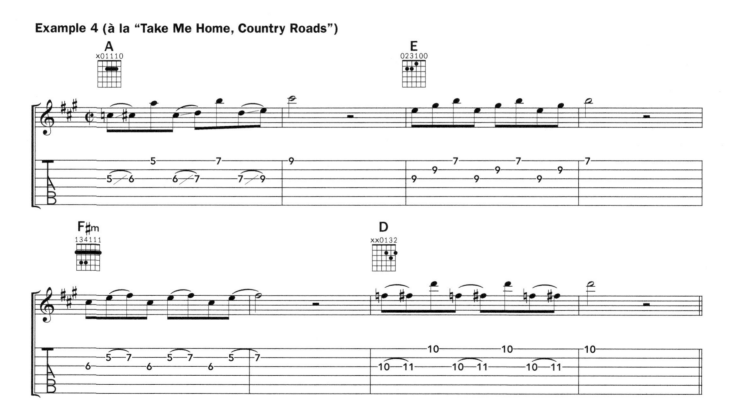

In "Sunshine," Denver capoed at the third fret (again playing a 12-string) and used shapes and picking patterns similar to those in **Examples 5** and **6**. Be sure to use the G fingering shown, with your third and fourth fingers, since that'll facilitate the shift to C—keep the latter digit in place on string 1 for both chords. When you switch to the C chord in Ex. 5, play the open fourth string with your index finger while your thumb picks the fifth-string C, and quickly hammer your second finger onto fret 2 of string 4. Ex. 6 shows the type of ascending chord pattern used in the second section of the verse. On the Am7 and D7/F# chords in both Exs. 5 and 6, pick the top two strings simultaneously with your middle and ring fingers.

Example 5 (à la "Sunshine on My Shoulders")
Capo III

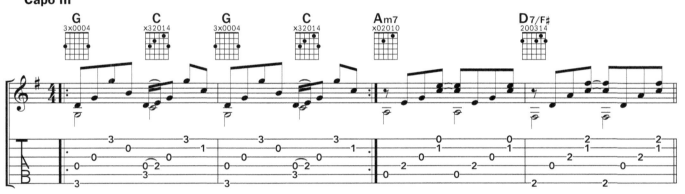

Example 6

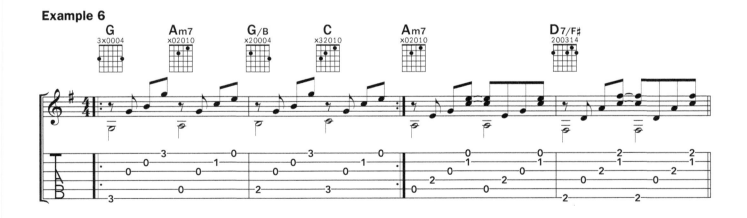

GOOD TO BE BACK HOME

The next two examples come from Denver's *Back Home Again* album, which won a string of hits and awards (and prompted the notorious incident when Charlie Rich, announcing the Entertainer of the Year at the 1975 Country Music Awards, lit Denver's name card on fire at the podium).

Example 7 is based on "Annie's Song," which Denver wrote for his first wife after an argument and reconciliation. The song came to him during a ride up a ski lift in his home of Aspen, Colorado—he often described figuring out song ideas in his head and then going to the guitar to learn them.

Example 7 (à la "Annie's Song")

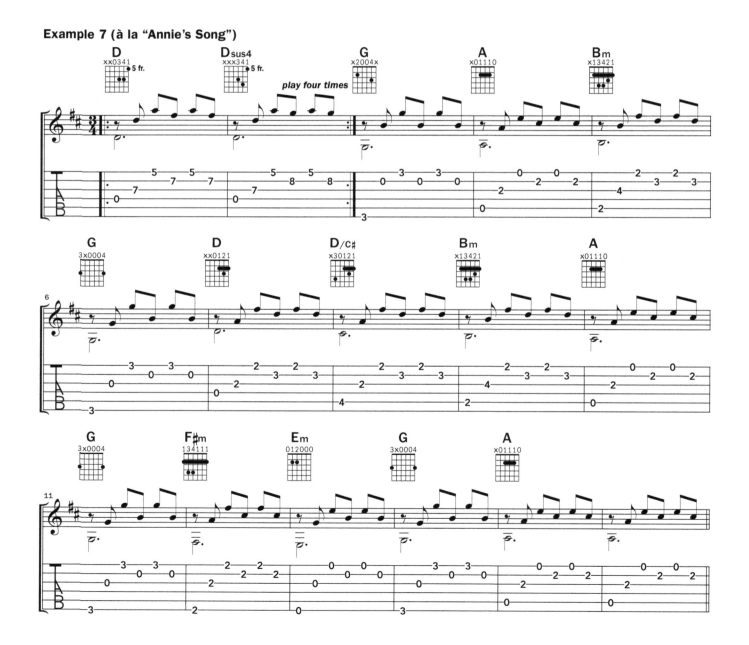

Originally picked on a 12-string, "Annie's Song" is in waltz time. In the first two measures of Ex. 7, play the D–Dsus4 move up at the fifth fret. On the final repetition of this pattern, you may find it helpful to substitute the open fourth string for the last note (the second-string G), to facilitate the shift down to the open G chord in the next measure. Using a first-finger barre for the A chord makes an efficient change to B minor in measures 4 and 5, and I've also suggested a barre version of an open D chord in measure 7 that allows you to keep the first and second fingers in place while moving to D/C♯ in the following bar.

The title track of *Back Home Again* is in a different vein than the other examples here, with a loping country/cowboy rhythm. In **Example 8**, play with a swing feel, where pairs of eighth notes sound like the first and third notes in a triplet. On each chord, alternate the bass on strings 6, 5, and 4 as shown, while picking the same pattern on top of the chords: third string with your index finger, top two strings together with your middle and ring fingers, and then third string again with your index.

Example 8 (à la "Back Home Again")

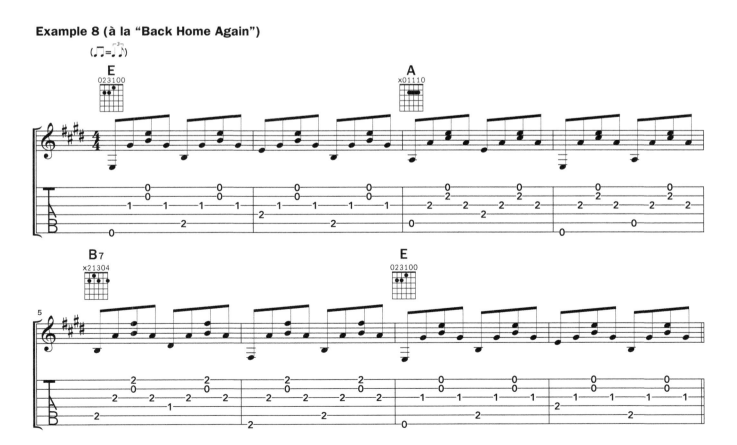

Like so many of Denver's songs, "Back Home Again" sounds effortless—both the melody and the words. As a songwriter he cultivated that quality, trying not to control or force the process but to let the song unfold. "There are times when I'd be struggling with a song," he wrote in *Take Me Home*, "and then when I'd get out of the way, the song would be there. In neon lights. Right in front of me. It's a way of looking, I think. What you need to see comes forward once you stop trying to see it."

FINGERSTYLE MELODIES

Denver's last Number One hit came in 1975 with "I'm Sorry," a tearjerker breakup ballad released on the album *Windsong*. Two decades later, he delivered a moving performance on the 1995 Wildlife Concert album and video, on which he opted to play a nylon-string—a nice match for the song's intimate mood.

"I'm Sorry" is a good example of how Denver used melodic hooks in his guitar parts to tie a song together. In the final volume of his Homespun video series, Pete Huttlinger built on Denver's melodic picking to turn "I'm Sorry" into a sweet instrumental. (Huttlinger, a fingerstyle master as well as an in-demand Nashville sideman, passed away in 2016 after a series of strokes—like Denver, he was only in his 50s.)

The first two measures of **Example 9** are based on the intro/interlude of "I'm Sorry." Rather than using an alternating bass pattern, pick bass notes only on beats 1 and 3; create a descending line by altering the Gmaj7 chord first to G6 and then to G. For simplicity, don't bother fretting the first or fifth strings in the G chord during the intro; just hold down the notes you actually need.

In measure 4, while holding down the G shape, add an A note on the third string and then a C on the second string at the end of the measure. These notes set up the change to the A minor chord and also anticipate the melody—the kind of small, elegant detail that was characteristic of Denver's style.

Example 9 (à la "I'm Sorry")

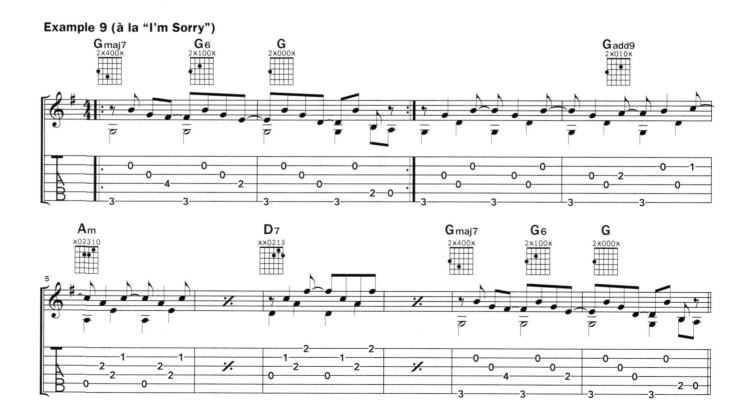

WRITING FOR THE WORLD

In early 2019, some new Denver music came to light, as the band Railroad Earth released *The John Denver Letters*, featuring two new songs, "If You Will Be My Lady" and "Through the Night," on which front man Todd Sheaffer set to music some rediscovered Denver lyrics. Both are lovely settings that sit comfortably alongside the Denver songs that have been circulating now for decades.

"Through the Night" opens with a soft fingerpicking melody and these lines:

Here beneath the starry sky
I lay me down to rest
Peace around me, peace within
For this, my life is blessed

As the song proceeds, the lyrics come back around and replace "I" with "you":

Here beneath the starry sky, love
Lay yourself to rest
Peace around you, peace within
For this, your life is blessed

In terms of the mood and the message, it's a perfect John Denver moment—a simple, personal expression of gratitude that opens up to include anyone listening or singing along. Utterly uncynical and hard to resist.   AG

WIKIMEDIA PHOTO, VIA ISLAND RECORDS

Things Behind the Sun

The Inner Workings of Nick Drake's Idiosyncratic Guitar Style   By Adam Perlmutter

Nick Drake achieved scant commercial success in his brief lifetime, but after he overdosed on antidepressants in his childhood bedroom in 1974, at the age of 26, the British singer-songwriter became a veritable cult hero, venerated equally by musicians, critics, and fans. His music has now long been a rich source of inspiration to a diverse range of artists, from singer-songwriters like Elton John and Norah Jones to jazz musicians such as pianist Brad Mehldau and vocalist Lizz Wright.

Much has certainly been made about Drake's reclusive persona, as well as his intelligent, impressionistic lyrics—he had been an English student in Cambridge—and his haunting voice. As a guitarist, Drake was similarly remarkable, both prodigious and inventive. While clearly inspired by British contemporaries like Bert Jansch and John Renbourn, Drake developed his own voice based on a use of unusual

tunings and strategic capo placement, to say nothing of a penchant for mixing folk and jazz strains in quietly thrilling ways.

The unorthodox tunings made it possible for Drake to create complex harmonies from one- and two-fingered chord shapes, freeing him to concentrate on his highly detailed picking patterns. In the process, he often spun a dense contrapuntal web that was as integral to his songs as his lyrics and vocals—each tune a revelation.

In this lesson we'll look under the microscope at the guitar parts to eight songs from Drake's three studio albums—*Five Leaves Left* (1969), *Bryter Layter* (1971), and *Pink Moon* (1972)—grouped in four different tunings.

This feature originally appeared in the March/April 2019 issue of Acoustic Guitar *magazine.*

STANDARD IN TUNING ONLY

Though known by guitarists for his unusual tunings, Drake did in fact play a bunch of songs in standard tuning, among them, "River Man" and "Things Behind the Sun." The former, which is the inspiration for **Example 1**, appears on *Five Leaves Left* (the title a reference to a refill warning in packs of Rizla rolling papers) and is an excellent example of the singer-songwriter's deft approach to harmony.

Though the song is in the key of A minor (sounding as C minor, due to a capo at the third fret), it starts off on a sunny note, and a colorful one at that. As depicted in the intro (bar 1), instead of a basic open-A chord, Drake opted for the more flavorful Aadd9. But the mood darkens at the onset of the verse (bar 2), with the introduction of the tonic minor chord, Am(add9). The verse winds its way back to Aadd9 before returning to Am(add9) on the repeat—a clever move lending emotional heft, reinforced by the original recording's deep string arrangement.

To play Ex. 1, hold down each chord shape for its full duration, picking the bass notes on strings 5 and 6 with your thumb and the chords above with your index, middle, and ring fingers. Note that the song is in 5/4—or five quarter notes per measure—a meter not usually associated with popular music, the jazz pianist Dave Brubeck's crossover hit "Take Five" being a notable exception. If it's easier, you can think of this instead as alternating bars of 3/4 and 2/4. Try playing along with the original recording to copy its characteristic gait.

Example 1 (à la "River Man")
Capo III

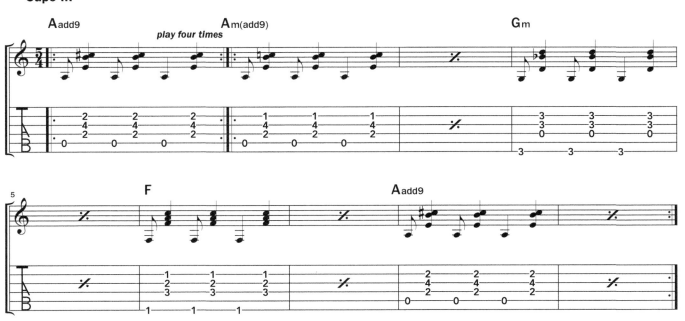

"Things Behind the Sun," from *Pink Moon*, starts off on a harmonically ambiguous chord, Asus2 (sounding as C#sus2 because of a capo at the fourth fret). But the song's dark minor mood is firmly established with the introduction of an Am chord. The notation here (**Example 2**) takes its cue from the song's intro (bars 2–6), which also forms the foundation of the verse.

The picking hand plays a fairly involved role in Ex. 2, so it's important to avoid excessive tension in that hand. The passage, with its syncopations, is also highly rhythmic, so you'll want to feel it with precision. It might be useful to subdivide—that is, to count the music in eighth notes, rather than quarters, as you normally would in 4/4 time. Be sure, too, to take a moment to listen closely to the interesting harmonies, especially the movement between the E and the F6/9(#4).

Example 2 (à la "Things Behind the Sun")
Capo IV

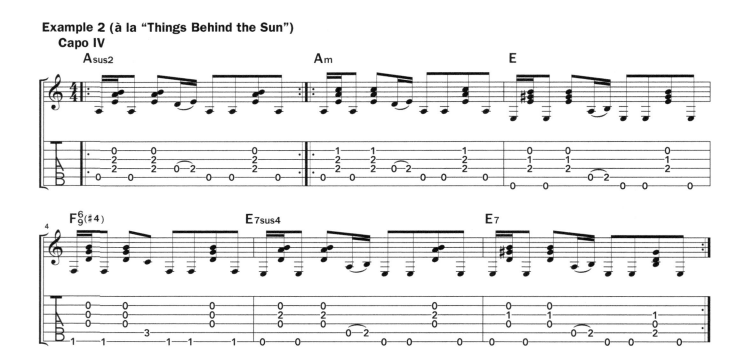

A SLIGHT WRINKLE

In two of his tunes, "Cello Song" and "The Thoughts of Mary Jane," which sit alongside each other on the B side of *Five Leaves Left*, Drake used a tuning that represents only a small deviation from the norm—low to high, E A D F♯ B E—the third string down a half step from standard. But this slight adjustment makes for some beautifully different effects.

Example 3 is based on a portion of the intro to "Cello Song." Throughout, a thumb-picked open A string (sounding as E♭), played in steady quarter notes, lends a driving feel. The first eight bars are based on the IV chord, A7, but there's plenty of variation to be had as the melody notes work their way up the A Mixolydian mode (A B C♯ D E F♯ G). On the original recording, Drake plays this part at an impressively brisk clip, one that's best to work up to slowly. When you're practicing the figure, pay close attention to where the upper and lower notes fall simultaneously (like on beats 1 and 4 of bar 1). For the A7 measures, use your second and first fingers to stop the notes at frets 2 and 1, respectively, and go for smoothness and rhythmic precision throughout.

Example 3 (à la "Cello Song")
Tuning: E A D F♯ B E, Capo VI

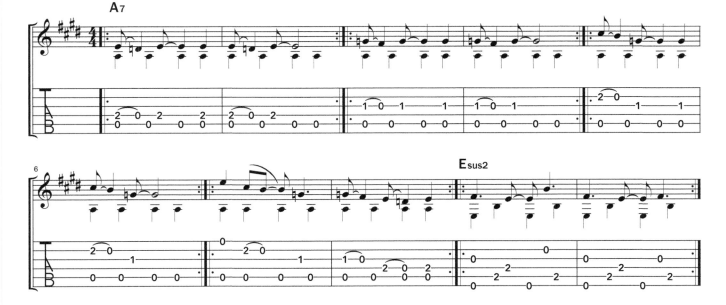

Many fans regard Drake as a dark and mysterious song-writer, but "The Thoughts of Mary Jane" reveals a brighter side. The intro and verse sections of this song are the bench-mark for **Example 4**, with its poignant harmonies and rolling arpeggios. Key to playing this passage successfully is doing so gently, with an even picking attack between your thumb, index, and ring fingers, and smoothly. Seek out the most efficient fretting fingerings, as well. For instance, I recommend playing the Amaj7 with fingers 1, 2, and 3 on strings 4, 3, and 2, respectively. That way, all you have to do is lift your second finger to access the subsequent A6 chord, and then, with your third finger still on string 2, you can grab string 4 at fret 1 with your first finger, to form the B9/A chord.

Example 4 (à la "The Thoughts of Mary Jane")
Tuning: E A D F♯ B E, Capo VI

TUNING DOWN

In songs like "Hazey Jane I," "Hazey Jane II," "Which Will," and "Pink Moon," Drake used a unique slackened tuning, lowest string to highest, C G C F C E, the open strings of which form a rich Cadd4 chord. To get into this tuning from standard, lower string 6 by two whole steps and strings 5, 4, and 3 by a whole step each; raise string 2 by a half step. If you want to spend any amount of time in this tuning, it would be optimal to use heavy strings, but it should work well enough with light or medium strings.

"Hazey Jane I," off of *Bryter Layter*, begins with a flurry of notes on the acoustic guitar, supported by bass guitar, strings, and percussion. **Example 5** is in the style of the guitar part, in which a series of jazzy chords are punctuated with slurs between single fretted notes and their corresponding open strings. This is a formidable figure, so if needed, isolate any problematic areas, like the pull-offs and hammer-ons in the two-beat pickup measure and elsewhere, until you have perfected them.

Throughout, pick the four-note chords with your thumb, index, middle, and ring fingers, or strum them briskly with your thumb or, alternatively, with your index finger. If, by the way, these chords feel awkward to pick, you can eliminate the lowest note in each voicing, for example, the fourth-string D on the Dm9 chord. Whichever picking approach you choose, in order to pull off Ex. 5, you'll need to transition seamlessly between the single-note and strummed portions, and the best way to confirm that you're doing so is to use a metronome.

Example 5 (à la "Hazey Jane I")
Tuning: C G C F C E, Capo II

On "Which Will," from *Pink Moon*, the foundation of which informs **Example 6**, Drake took a similar approach to "Hazey Jane I," embellishing single-note nuggets with chordal strums to create a texturally and harmonically sophisticated accompaniment. When playing Ex. 6, unlike on the previous examples, you should forego a capo; that way you can enjoy the extended low end provided by the tuning, as well as match Drake's original studio recording.

As with "Hazey Jane I," practice the figure slowly, isolating any tricky spots before stitching everything together, and carefully count the rhythms throughout.

Example 6 (à la "Which Will")
Tuning: C G C F C E

LOWER STILL

Drake used an even more slackened tuning—B E B E B E, the open strings forming a Bsus4 or E5 chord—in songs like "Man in a Shed" and "Fly." From standard tuning, lower string 3 by a minor third, such that it sounds an octave lower than the first string. Do the same with string 4, which should then be an octave below string 2. Next, lower strings 5 and 6 by a fifth each, or an octave below strings 3 and 4, respectively.

On "Man in a Shed" (*Five Leaves Left*), Drake made the most of a two-finger chord grip, fretted on strings 4 and 5 alongside the open strings, as approximated in **Example 7**. To play this figure, start by stopping the fourth and fifth strings at fret 4 with your second and third fingers—the same shape that you'll use until the B5 (sounds as D5) in bar 2, then resume at the beginning of bar 3. Be sure to appreciate the colorful harmonies that result from the interaction between this shape and the open strings as you slide down in half steps: Emaj7/G♯, Em7/G, F♯7sus4, etc.

A couple of things to look out for: In bars 1, 2, and 5, there's a chord change not on the expected beat 2, but on the and of beat 1, so be sure to move the shape in time. You'll find a half-step bend in bar 6—with your third finger, reinforced by your first and second fingers on string 2, nudge the string toward the ceiling such that it matches the pitch of the note found one fret higher. If this a problem, just slide up to that pitch. Also, as shown in the swing indication at the top of the example, play the eighth notes not evenly as written, but long-short, for jazzy rhythmic effect.

Example 7 (à la "Man in a Shed")
Tuning: B E B E B E, Capo III

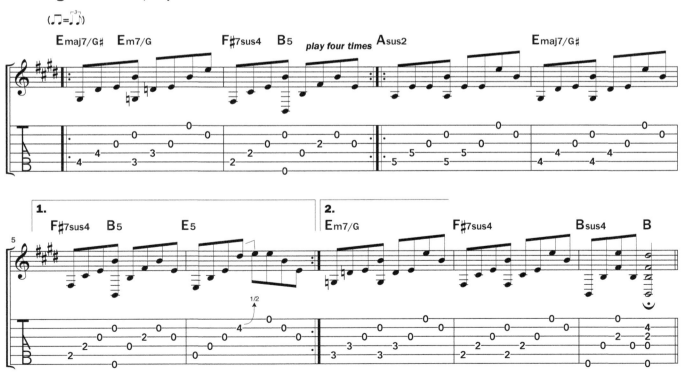

Heard on *Bryter Layter* and also appearing on the soundtrack to the 2001 film *The Royal Tenenbaums*, "Fly" found Drake further exploring textures involving fretted notes pitted against open strings in the tuning. The studio recording of the song, by the way, features one of the grandest arrangements in Drake's body of work, in which the singer-songwriter's steel-string guitar is gilded with Baroque-style viola and harpsichord, courtesy of the Velvet Underground's John Cale.

Example 8 is inspired by the intro and verse sections from "Fly," which essentially form the bulk of the song. In bars 1 and 2, a descending line within the E major scale (sounds as G#/Ab) is played in second position—remember, use your first, third, and fourth fingers on the second-, fourth-, and fifth-fret notes, respectively—and each fretted note is paired with two adjacent open strings, lending a kind of pastoral effect.

If you've tackled the other figures in this lesson, then Ex. 8 should be fairly accessible. A potentially tricky spot is the chord change, to B5 from Emaj7/D#, between bars 6 and 7.

A little fretting-hand efficiency is in order here. Play the Asus2 in bar 5 with your second finger on string 5 and your fourth finger on string 2, sliding that shape down one fret for the Emaj7/D# chord in the following measure. That way, you'll be easily prepared to play the B5 chord in bar 7— just keep your second finger on string 5 and add your third finger to string 3.

Remember, of course, to take a moment to absorb the beautiful textures and harmonies facilitated by this nonstandard tuning. But consider that ultimately the biggest takeaways from scrutinizing Drake's guitar style aren't necessarily the specific tunings, chord progressions, and picking patterns, but rather a welcome spirit of adventurousness and an exploration of the fretboard far beyond stock fingerings and patterns. **AG**

Example 8 (à la "Fly")
Tuning: B E B E B E, Capo IV

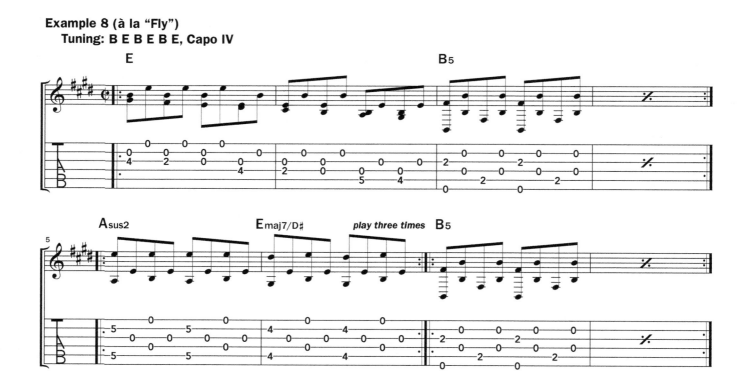

WIKIMEDIA PHOTO

Hidden in Plain Sight

Bob Dylan Just May Be the Best Acoustic Guitarist You've Never Bothered to Notice

By Adam Levy

First and foremost, Bob Dylan is a wordsmith. His lyrics are the reason people still buy his records—old and new—and continue to flock to his concerts. His way with language is why every generation of songwriters since the early 1960s has studied his work. Dylan's words are what kept his 2004 memoir, *Chronicles*, on *The New York Times* bestseller list for 19 weeks. Yet, for all the accolades Dylan has earned as a writer, there is an aspect of his artistry that often gets overlooked: his great acoustic guitar playing. It's been there all along, for anyone who cared to notice.

This feature originally appeared in the December 2016 issue of Acoustic Guitar *magazine.*

On the 50th anniversary of *John Wesley Harding*, an album that signaled the beginning of a seven-year period in which Dylan would record *The Basement Tapes* and release a half-dozen largely acoustic albums, *AG* decided to showcase his acoustic side. Of course, Dylan has expressed his acoustic side throughout his nearly seven-decade-long career. Let's take a closer look at some of Dylan's deceptive chord moves, his fluency with standard and nonstandard tunings, and his knack for constant reinvention. The music examples are mostly drawn from his early work. He's made a lot of great music in the ensuing years, of course, but his relatively spare early recordings are where the fundamentals of Dylan's style are most easily heard and appreciated.

DO LOOK BACK

In the early 1960s, at the beginning of his career, Dylan was an unabashed folkie. He wrote and sang of landmark news events such as the assassination of civil-rights activist Medgar Evers ("Only a Pawn in Their Game"), warmongering ("Masters of War"), and social justice ("A Hard Rain's A-Gonna Fall"). While honing his own material, the young artist also took it upon himself to become a walking compendium of traditional American styles, absorbing song after song. On his eponymous 1962 Columbia Records debut, featuring just his voice, harmonica, and solo acoustic guitar, Dylan showcases his ease with such forms—on the gospel song "In My Time of Dying," for example, and Blind Lemon Jefferson's blues "See That My Grave Is Kept Clean."

Columbia released Dylan's second record, *The Freewheelin' Bob Dylan*, just a year later. It was a huge leap forward, artistically, featuring a dozen original songs—including the instant classics "Blowin' in the Wind" and "Don't Think Twice, It's All Right"—as well as the traditional "Corrina, Corrina" (featuring the ornamental second guitar of studio ace Bruce Langhorne). *Freewheelin'* closely followed the sonic template of its predecessor—vocal, harmonica, and mostly solo acoustic guitar (often strummed close to the bridge to give a percussive effect)—yet Dylan's guitar work is more confident and more varied than before.

His continued development is evident on *The Times They Are A-Changin'*, in 1964, with Dylan employing a wider variety of strumming patterns and some lovely fingerpicking on "One Too Many Mornings" (more on this song later). *Another Side of Bob Dylan*, also released in '64, finds Dylan once again in solo troubadour mode. Featuring "My Back Pages" and "It Ain't Me Babe," the entire album, incredibly, was recorded in just one long, late-night session.

In 1965, Dylan did something that many fans and critics never saw coming—he went electric, donning a Stratocaster at the Newport Folk Festival. Backed by electric guitarist Michael Bloomfield and other members of the Paul Butterfield Blues Band, Dylan's amped-up set caused an uproar. That same year, he released not one but two albums pulsing with rock-and-roll energy—*Bringing It All Back Home*, in March, then *Highway 61 Revisited* five months later. The double-LP *Blonde on Blonde* was released in May of '66 and features several of the songs that would later become Dylan's calling cards, including "Visions of Johanna" and "Just Like a Woman." He returned to Nashville and released *John Wesley Harding* at the end of 1967. Though the album features a small backing band—bass, drums, and occasional pedal-steel guitar—the tone is spartan compared with the three energized releases that preceded it.

HIGHER & HIGHER

Dylan's acoustic guitar chimes clearly through-out each song on *John Wesley Harding*. He sometimes achieves this by using a capo to move his voicings farther up the fretboard than you might expect—presumably so his chords won't get lost in the mix. The higher-register guitar also frees up more latitude for his voice.

"I Dreamed I Saw St. Augustine" is a good example of his use of a capo on *John Wesley Harding*. The song is in the key of F major. Dylan could've played it in E with his capo at the first fret, or in D with the capo at the third fret—but he plays the song in C with the capo at the fifth fret. (The recording also features a second acoustic-guitar track, much quieter in the mix, played in a lower position.) **Example 1** is in the style of "I Dreamed I Saw St. Augustine."

Similarly, the album's title track is in the key of F and played in C with a capo at the fifth fret. The track "As I Went Out One Morning" is in the key of F♯ minor, played in D minor, with a capo at the fourth fret. An interesting aspect of the specific voicings in Ex. 1 is that two of them—F/C and D7/A—have the fifth in the bass instead of the root. (The note C is the fifth degree of the chord F; A is the fifth of D7.) Dylan has used this inverted harmony repeatedly throughout his repertoire.

NEVER THE SAME WAY

Unlike many singer-songwriters, Dylan has never been precious about performing his songs live the same way he recorded them. "Desolation Row" is a classic example. On the original studio recording—from *Highway 61 Revisited*—he plays this epic three-chord song in drop-C tuning (C A D G B E), with a capo at the fourth fret, sounding in E. **Example 2a** is similar to the first four bars of each verse section of "Desolation Row."

This particular tuning and capo setup gives Dylan a sonorous low-C bass note, even though he's four frets above open position. It also makes it easy to grab the harmonically ambiguous Cadd4 by adding his fourth finger, which he does consistently on this version of "Desolation Row." (It's worth noting that the *Highway 61 Revisited*

Example 1 (à la "I Dreamed I Saw St. Augustine")
Capo V

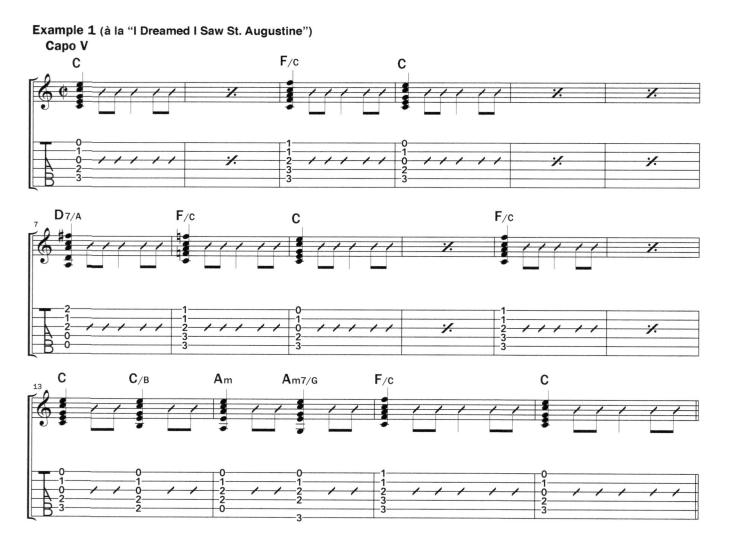

recording of the song features Nashville session guitarist Charlie McCoy, who provides tasty acoustic-guitar fills from start to finish.)

Dylan played at Manchester Free Trade Hall in the UK during his 1966 world tour. A bootleg recording of the show has circulated ever since, with the venue misidentified as the "Royal Albert Hall." Dylan's acoustic and electric sets from that night were officially released in 1998 as *The Bootleg Series Vol. 4: Bob Dylan Live 1966*, The "Royal Albert Hall" Concert. His version of "Desolation Row" from that performance is markedly different from the one on *Highway 61 Revisited*. He plays the song at a slightly brighter tempo, in the key of D, in drop-D tuning. (Interestingly, he uses that drop-C tuning—with capo at the fifth fret—for a downtempo

rendition of "Just Like a Woman," but not for "Desolation Row." **Example 2b** is inspired by Dylan's "Desolation Row" verses as played at that show in '66.

When Dylan performed "Desolation Row" during his 1994 appearance on *MTV Unplugged* (later released as a live album), he took a different approach to the song altogether. Here, he's in the key of D, in standard tuning. Backed by a five-piece band—including the tasteful Bucky Baxter on Dobro—Dylan pares down his part to nothing more than palm-muted power chords, not unlike **Example 2c**.

Example 2a (à la "Desolation Row")
Tuning: C A D G B E, Capo IV

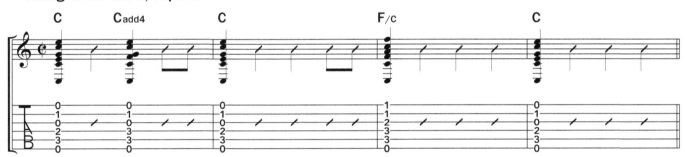

Example 2b
Tuning: D A D G B E

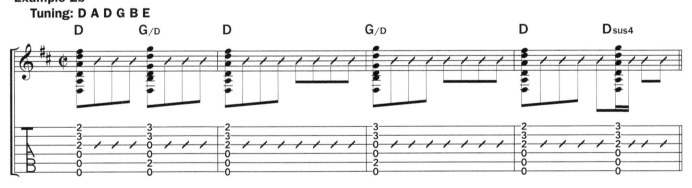

Example 2c
Standard Tuning

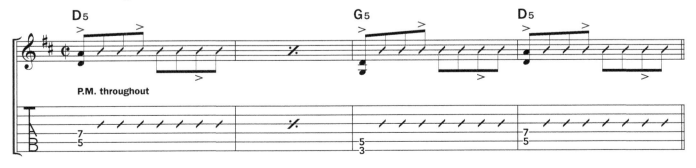

PET SOUNDS

It's not unusual to find Dylan using and reusing a limited array of his favorite harmonic elements within each album. These may include particular tunings, chord progressions, chord voicings, and such. That's part of his genius as a player and songwriter—he can take simple musical ideas and rework them in seemingly endless combinations.

There are ten guitar songs on *Another Side of Bob Dylan* (an 11th track, "Black Crow Blues," is played on piano.) Half of these ten are in the key of G, played in open position, using rudimentary chords. The album's rollicking opening song—"All I Really Want to Do"—is in G with a capo at the second fret, again using common chords. Three of the remaining songs—"My Back Pages," "I Don't Believe You," and the ironically titled "Ballad in Plain D"—are played in C, using the capo for transposition to nearby keys. "To Ramona" is also played in C, without capo. That's a lot of juice squeezed from just two humble pieces of fruit: the key of G and the key of C.

The main thing that sets each of these songs apart from all other three-chord songs is their knockout lyrical punch. However, Dylan's guitar work is rarely as straightforward as it seems upon first listen. If you take the time to really check out what he's playing behind his broadsides and ballads, you may be shocked by the nuances his hands are capable of. Take, for example, the aforementioned songs in the key of C from *Another Side*. On all of these, the home-base C chord is nearly always played as C/G (**Example 3**). Placing the chord's fifth (G) in the bass, instead of the expected root (C), gives the chord an expansive quality.

Example 3

Dylan uses a similar sonority on "Blowin' in the Wind," from *The Freewheelin' Bob Dylan*. Played in G, with the capo at seventh fret, the song sounds in the key of D (**Example 4**, in the style of "Blowin'"). The chord in bars 11–12 includes the open first string (E), giving the B minor-triad a little extra bite. Subtle? Yes. But without this stepwise bass motion, the song would sound like a million other I–IV–V–I songs.

To hear that fifth-in-the-bass voicing in another context, check out **Example 5**, loosely based on Dylan's "I Am a Lonesome Hobo," from *John Wesley Harding*. In this protracted blues (a 19-bar cycle in lieu of the standard 12), Dylan propels the music forward by never letting the I chord (G) settle, toggling between G and C/G instead. The effect is kind of Stones-y, as if Mick Jagger and Keith Richards had decided to be folkies for a day.

Example 4 (à la "Blowin' in the Wind")
Capo VII

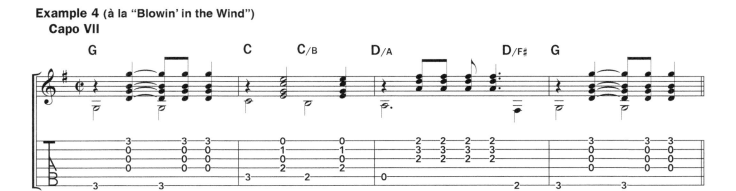

Example 5 (à la "I Am a Lonesome Hobo")

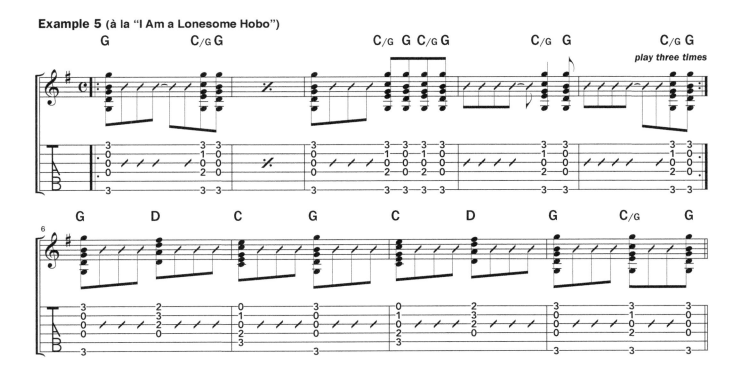

On "It Ain't Me Babe"—from *Another Side*—Dylan uses that bottom-heavy chord form again. Check out **Example 6**, inspired by "It Ain't Me Babe." Bars 7–10 could be played as a static G chord; in this example, however, as in Dylan's original, there's a syncopated move to C/G (bar 7, beat 4). That C/G blurs the line between the I (G) and IV (C) chords. C/G reappears four bars before the end of this example. There are a few other unorthodox chord voicings worth looking at here. Right off the bat, in bars 1 and 2, the D chord is rendered by fretting a common C chord two frets higher than usual, which lets the open third string (G) rub against the fretted F♯ on the fourth string. The Bm chord in bar 11 includes the open first string (E), giving the chord a little extra bite. As in the previous example, C/G reappears here four bars before the end.

Example 6 (à la "It Ain't Me Babe")

In 1993, nearly 30 years after *Another Side*, Dylan released an equally powerful solo-acoustic record, *World Gone Wrong*. On the title track, the songwriter works his understated magic again. As he did in "I Am a Lonesome Hobo," Dylan builds "World Gone Wrong" on an expanded blues form. In this sort of atmosphere, only three simple chords are needed to get the job done, but that wouldn't be very Dylan. Look at **Example 7**, inspired by "World Gone Wrong." Notice the curious Cadd4 chord on the fourth beat of bars 2, 4, and 6? It's similar to the chord you saw in Ex. 2a (bar 1, beat 3). This particular voicing also could be called C/F, as all three notes of the C triad (C, E, and G) are present above the bottommost F note. Regardless of the nomenclature, this chord upends the harmony every time it comes around.

E7/D, the second "mystery chord" in "World Gone Wrong," comes into play in bar 4. With its ear-tugging tritone interval (G#–D), the chord sounds unresolved and misplaced. As in Dylan's original, the E7/D here seems to be justified when you get to the F chord in bar 5. One more harmonic oddity appears in bars 15 and 16. It's unusual to find any major seven chord in a blues song; in this case, it's an unexpected chord in an unexpected voicing, with the open second string (B) rubbing against the fretted C a half step away on the third string.

Example 7 (à la "World Gone Wrong")
Capo II

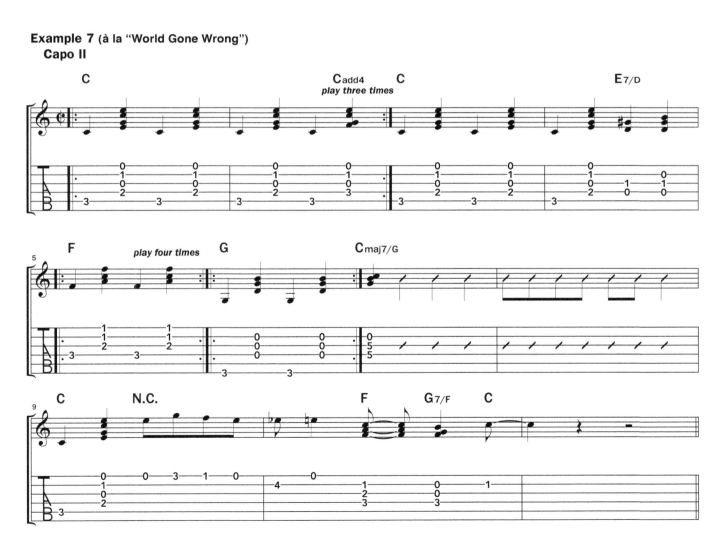

ARE WE TUNING, BOB?

As interested as Dylan is in the novel effects of unusual chord voicings, it's no surprise he uses alternate tunings from time to time. His early work features several songs in drop D (D A D G B E), including "A Hard Rain's A-Gonna Fall" and "Mr. Tambourine Man." He also favored double-drop D (D A D G B D), as you can hear in "Ballad of Hollis Brown," and drop C (C A D G B E), in "It's All Over Now, Baby Blue," "Sad-Eyed Lady of the Lowlands," "Desolation Row," and other songs. In addition to those, Dylan has used a handful of open-chord tunings, among them open G (D G D G B D), used on "I Was Young When I Left Home," and open D (D A D F♯ A D) or open E (E B E G♯ B E), which he used extensively on *Blood on the Tracks*. The final few examples in this lesson illustrate some of these tunings.

Example 8 is styled after Dylan's take on the folk-blues tune "Corrina, Corrina," from *The Freewheelin' Bob Dylan*. It is played in open D (D A D F♯ A D) with a capo at the third fret, sounding in the key of F. The chord voicings in bar 2 reprise two Dylan-centric moves that you've seen throughout this lesson—G/D is a triad with its fifth in the bass; Aadd4 is akin to the unsettled (add4) chords used earlier, in Ex. 2a and Ex. 7. Note that the guitar part is more active in bars 3 and 4—in between the vocal phrase—and less active while Dylan is singing. This helps the music feel conversational, with the voice and guitar exchanging phrases back and forth as the song rolls along.

Example 8 (à la "Corrina Corrina")
Tuning: D A D F♯ A D, Capo III

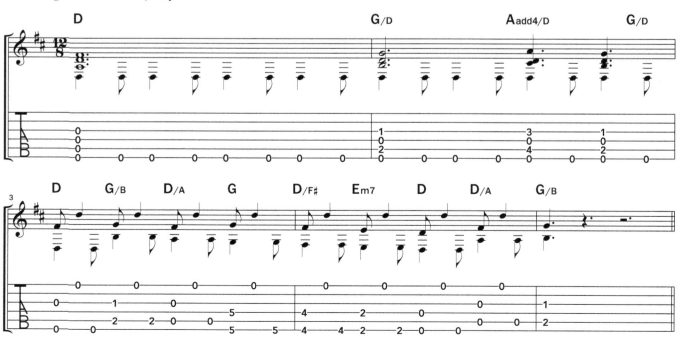

On *Blood on the Tracks*, Dylan pushed this same tuning style (though in open E) far beyond the folk-blues idiom, playing each of the album's ten songs in the same tuning (sometimes transposed, via capo). "Simple Twist of Fate" is an example of how he developed a chordal vocabulary rich enough to match his narrative prowess. In **Example 9** you can trace some of his "Simple Twist of Fate" maneuvers. (This example is written in open D with a capo at the second

fret, so that you don't have to tighten your strings up to open E.) What's so different from the previous example is that this time the I chord is not made by simply sounding the open strings; instead, it is played a few frets above open position, in two variations.

Example 9 (à la "Simple Twist of Fate")
Tuning: D A D F♯ A D, Capo II

In bar 1, the D chord's fifth (A) is doubled on the fretted third string and on the open second string. Note the slightly different harmony in bar 11, where the D chord's third (F#) is doubled instead of the fifth. This two-finger version of D makes it a little easier to get to the next two-finger chord shape, the colorful Dmaj9. Check out the two deceptively simple moves in bars 12 and 14. Lifting your finger off the second string in bar 12 changes G/B to Gadd9/B, while the same lift converts A9sus4 to A7sus4 two bars later.

Finally, **Example 10** is reminiscent of "One Too Many Mornings," from *The Times They Are A-Changin'*. The open-A tuning (E A C# E A C#) is novel, one that Dylan rarely uses. You may be unfamiliar with it—most players are—but it's pretty intuitive once you get a few simple shapes under your fingers. Once again, the use of A/E (triad with fifth

in the bass) has Dylan's fingerprints on it. The harmony in the last few bars (Bm11–A/C#–Bm11) is also elusive. There's a slight similarity between the melody and structure of this song and that of the title track. Thanks to the alternate tuning in "One Too Many Mornings" ("The Times They Are A-Changin'" is in standard) and a burbling fingerpicking pattern ("The Times" is strummed), the two songs have an entirely different feel.

As Dylan has shown time and again, it's not the broad strokes that make a song special. It's the details. Some details aren't meant to be noticed, but they can shine like diamonds once you know where to look.   AG

Example 10 (à la "One Too Many Mornings")
Tuning: E A C# E A C#, Capo III

A Singular Voice

Inside Joni Mitchell's Inventive Guitar Style

By Jeffrey Pepper Rodgers

This feature originally appeared in the February 2019 issue of Acoustic Guitar *magazine.*

PAUL C BABIN PHOTO

The first and last time Joni Mitchell tried to learn guitar in a conventional way, she was just starting to play—swept up in the folk revival of the early '60s—and picked up a Pete Seeger instructional record.

"I went straight to the Cotten picking," she told me in an *Acoustic Guitar* interview back in 1996. "Your thumb went from the sixth string, fifth string, sixth string, fifth string. . . . I couldn't do that, so I ended up playing mostly the sixth string but banging it into the fifth string. So Elizabeth Cotten definitely is an influence; it's me not being able to play like her."

Fortunately for all of us, what Mitchell accomplished on guitar, instead of copping Cotten's fingerpicking style, was something far more significant: She learned to play like herself—and no one else. Using an ever-changing array of alternate tunings to generate unusual harmonies, and a unique harp-like picking style, Mitchell reinvented the guitar as a vehicle for accompaniment and songwriting. The evolution of her guitar style is inseparable from her journey as one of the defining singer-songwriters of her generation.

In the past, trying to decipher how Mitchell created those lush guitar sounds on seminal albums like *Court and Spark* or *Hejira* involved some real detective work, but nowadays her guitar work is much better documented.

The official Mitchell website offers an exhaustive library of transcriptions, many YouTube lessons are available, and after decades in development, the *Joni Mitchell Complete So Far . . .* guitar songbook (with tunings and shapes for 167 songs, and my 1996 *AG* cover story as the foreword) was finally published in 2014.

Even with all these resources, it is easy to become dazed and confused while exploring Mitchell's world of guitar—as I was just reminded when I picked up a guitar I'd left in the tuning B F D E A C (used in "Last Chance Lost" from *Turbulent Indigo*) and felt like I'd stepped into the *Twilight Zone*. The best way to study her style is step by step, progressing from the more folk-rooted songs of her first few albums to her later, jazzier music, and that's the aim of this lesson. For additional guidance, I reached out to Howard Wright, Sue Tierney, and Dave Blackburn—three Mitchell guitar obsessives who've contributed to the guitar sections of jonimitchell.com—as well as singer-songwriter Eric Andersen, who helped Mitchell get started on the open-tuning path.

Mitchell released her last studio album, *Shine*, in 2007, and has been mostly out of the public eye for the last decade, especially since suffering a brain aneurysm in 2015. She turned 75 in November, an event celebrated at a gala concert in Los Angeles with performances by Graham Nash, James Taylor, Chaka Khan, Emmylou Harris, Norah Jones, Los Lobos, and many more. So this is an apt time to explore the legacy of a pioneering guitarist whose music is a wellspring of ideas for going beyond standard approaches to the instrument.

STRUMMING IN OPEN D

Almost right out of the gate as a guitarist and songwriter, Mitchell started using alternate tunings; one likely reason she went in this direction, according to David Yaffe's recent biography, *Reckless Daughter*, is that tuning to an open chord made playing easier on her hands, weakened by childhood polio. Only a couple of her very early songs ("The Urge for Going," "Tin Angel") and late ones ("Harlem in Havana," "Shine") are in standard tuning.

Mitchell's tuning odyssey began in the mid-'60s, when she was living in Detroit and performing as a duo with her then-husband, Chuck Mitchell. One fateful night, Joni went to the local folk club Chessmate to hear Eric Andersen, who'd gotten into open tunings from slide players like Muddy Waters and Mississippi Fred McDowell.

"She hated playing guitar in standard tuning," Andersen recalls. "Standard tuning could be difficult—think learning and playing the F barre chord—and, in her case, boring, missing many musical regions she had in mind. In my show in Detroit I was playing in E, D, and G tunings. Afterwards we went to her lovely home. She was curious about these tunings, so I showed her. From there, the rest was history."

A good entry point into Mitchell's style is open D (D A D F A D), as heard on some of her most covered songs, such as "Big Yellow Taxi" and "Both Sides Now." She also strummed these songs, so the picking-hand technique is straightforward compared with what came later.

In the *Complete So Far* songbook, "Big Yellow Taxi" and "Both Sides Now," along with other songs from her early albums, are shown as open E (E B E G B E), which is the same as open D up a whole step. Since open E involves raising strings 5, 4, and 3 higher than standard, which could be inadvisable depending on the guitar and string gauge, I use open D and capo up to match the original keys.

In **Example 1**, strum through a progression based on "Conversation," from *Ladies of the Canyon*, using open D with a capo at the fourth fret. As in most Mitchell songs, there are only a few repeating shapes and lots of ringing open strings. For the F and E chords, use a one-finger barre at the third and second frets, respectively.

One of the beauties of open tunings is how they facilitate playing fretted notes high up the neck over open bass strings, widening the range of the instrument. Mitchell took advantage of this sound early on in "Chelsea Morning," another open D (or open E) strummer. In **Example 2**, based on the verse, start way up at the tenth and 12th frets (above the capo) on the high strings, then shift down the neck to play a one-finger A barre chord at the fifth fret. As

Example 1 (à la "Conversation")
Tuning: D A D F♯ A D, Capo IV

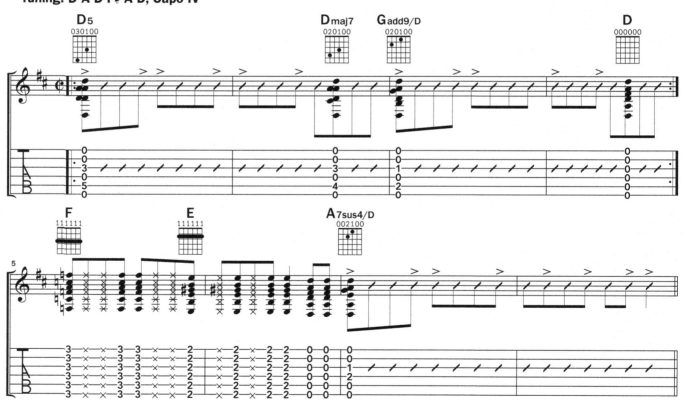

in Example 1, play open strings between chord shapes. **Example 3** shows a sweet passage based on the refrain ("Oh, won't you stay/ We'll put on the day…"), where the descending bass line adds a touch of bluesiness to an otherwise bright, major-sounding progression.

Even as Mitchell ventured into more radical tunings, she continued to come back to open D in songs such as "People's Parties" and "Amelia" (down a step from open D to open C: C G C E G C).

Example 2 (à la "Chelsea Morning" verse)
Tuning: D A D F# A D, Capo II

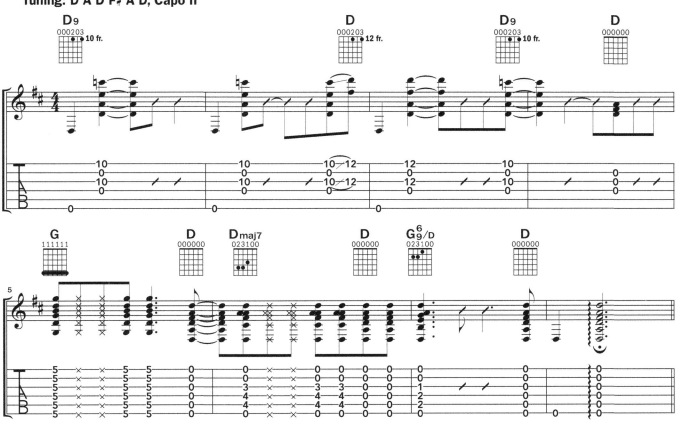

Example 3 (à la "Chelsea Morning" chorus)
Tuning: D A D Fs A D, Capo II

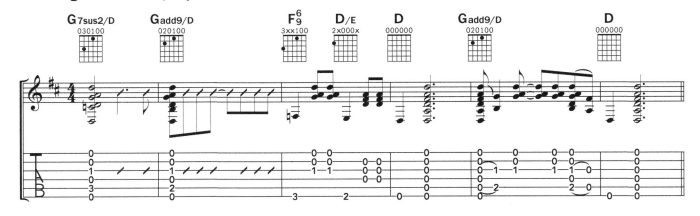

FINGERPICKING IN OPEN G

In her early songs, Mitchell also made use of the other common open tuning she learned from Andersen, open G (D G D G B D). One open-G classic is "The Circle Game," which had already been covered by Ian and Sylvia, Buffy Sainte-Marie, and Tom Rush before Mitchell released her own version on *Ladies of the Canyon* in 1970. As you can see in **Example 4**, based on the chorus, the shapes are simple but the fingerpicking pattern is a little tricky: It follows a syncopated 1-2-3/1-2-3/1-2 rhythm, with bass notes on each 1. Sue Tierney refers to the precise picking on songs like this as Mitchell's "music box fingerstyle." Practice the pattern just on the open G, as in measure 1, slowly at first. You may notice that the upper notes of the fingerpicking part hint at the melody; Mitchell's vocal and guitar are always closely intertwined.

Example 4 (à la "The Circle Game")
Tuning: D G D G B D, Capo IV

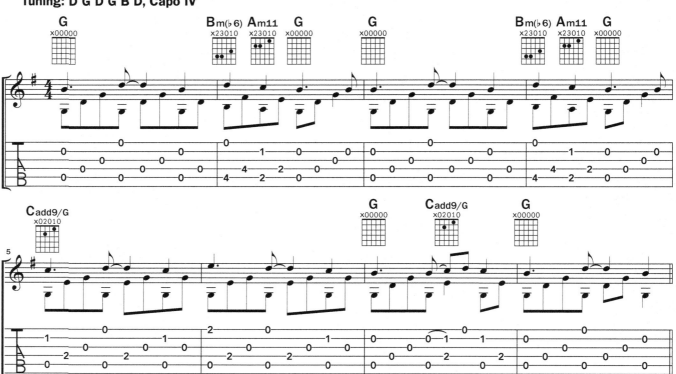

If you want to venture further in learning "The Circle Game," be aware that she actually reached over the bass side of the fretboard with her index finger for two barre shapes, as shown in **Example 5**.

Example 5
Tuning: D G D G B D, Capo IV

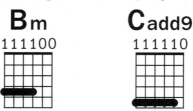

This is reminiscent of the thumb fretting technique of her contemporary Richie Havens, in his case using open-D tuning. For additional practice with open-G fingerpicking, play **Example 6**, based on "Little Green." In conjunction with the open tuning, the simple fingerings create some nice extended harmonies.

TUNING IN AND FINDING SHAPES

Especially starting with *For the Roses* (1972), Mitchell went off the charts in terms of tunings and picking technique. Some songs on the album use variations on open D (like "Barangrill," in the D7 tuning D A C F A D) or open G (like "For the Roses," G G D G B D, with the sixth string an octave below the fifth).

She used open G with the sixth string down to C on "Cold Blue Steel and Sweet Fire." In **Example 7**, shift from a bluesy bass riff to lush chords fretted on the middle strings and surrounded by open strings.

Example 6 (à la "Little Green")
Tuning: D G D G B D, Capo IV

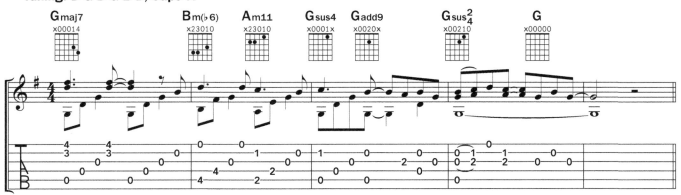

Example 7 (à la "Cold Blue Steel and Sweet Fire")
Tuning: C G D G B D

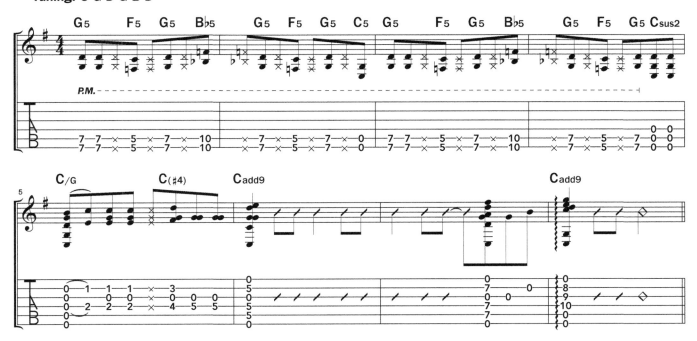

On *For the Roses*, a sign of things to come is "Woman of Heart and Mind," played in B F♯ C♯ E B D♯—that's a B major chord with the 9th and 11th added. Try it in **Example 8**, which for simplicity's sake uses this tuning a half step higher (C G D F C E). Fretting the middle strings up the neck creates some gorgeous sounds. Another Mitchell guitar gem in this tuning (the C version), and using similar shapes, is "Just Like This Train" from *Court and Spark*. Over time, Mitchell favored tunings like this that easily generate rich harmonies such as suspended, 6th, 7th, 9th, and 13th chord voicings.

Example 8 (à la "Woman of Heart and Mind")
Tuning: C G D F C E

For all the fanciness of the chord names, the shapes Mitchell used throughout her songs are remarkably simple and consistent—one-finger barres and a few recurring shapes like the one used for Fadd9 and D9 in Ex. 8. (For the record, though the chord grids show using four fingers for this shape, Mitchell herself often used her thumb to fret the sixth string.) The harmonic complexity is under the hood of the tunings, not from the fingerings. Here's how Mitchell described her approach to chord shapes: "Put it in a tuning and you've got three chords immediately—open, barre five, barre seven, and your higher octave, like half-fingering on the 12th," she said.

"Then you've got to find where your minors are and where the interesting colors are—that's the exciting part."

Though she used simple shapes overall, Mitchell rarely strummed them as block chords. She described the guitar as a mini orchestra, with the top strings as her horn section and the bottom three as cello and viola (and on albums like *Court and Spark*, she made these conceptions literal by doubling some of her horn-style guitar lines with actual horns and woodwinds). In many songs she used partial chords and played harmonized melodies on pairs of strings. You can hear this effect in **Example 9**, based on "Refuge of the Roads" (from *Hejira*, in the tuning C A C F A C). Play a melodic riff on the treble strings on top of one-finger barres at the seventh and fifth frets.

JONI MITCHELL HEJIRA

Example 9 (à la "Refuge of the Roads")
Tuning: C A C F A C

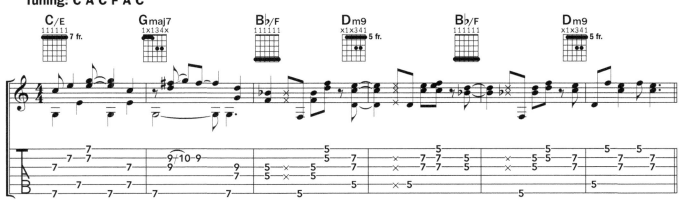

RIGHT-HAND BAND

One of the most challenging aspects of Mitchell's guitar style to emulate is the picking-hand technique that she favored from the mid-'70s onward—a blend of fingerstyle picking and strumming often described as a brush stroke. In Howard Wright's words, "Much of the time, she uses only her thumb for the lowest strings, with two or three fingers working together to strum partial chords on the other strings (with upstrokes), and individual fingers sometimes picking out phrases and melodic lines." Maintaining nails that extend beyond the fingertips, he adds, is essential for getting a clear tone on the upstrokes.

In addition to covering the low end, the thumb provides percussion with light slaps on the bass strings. As Mitchell put it, "A lot of my style is raking the chords and slapping it so that the bass string is almost more of a snare drum. It's sometimes quite atonal."

If you watch live videos of Mitchell—highly recommended to get a handle on this aspect of her style—notice the graceful, undulating motion of her right hand. "She has long, slender hands," says Dave Blackburn, "and she was able to drape them over the strings in a wonderfully relaxed way, with her picking direction very perpendicular to the strings using a perfect wrist arc."

Practice Mitchell's picking style in **Example 10**, based on her lesser-known gem "Night Ride Home," in the Cadd9 tuning C G D E G C. Pick bass notes with your thumb and upstrokes on the treble strings with your fingers, and drop your thumb gently onto the bass strings for a light slap, mostly on beat 2—an effect like a tap on the hi-hat. For inspiration, check YouTube for Mitchell's gorgeous solo rendition of "Night Ride Home" taped for Dutch national TV in 1988.

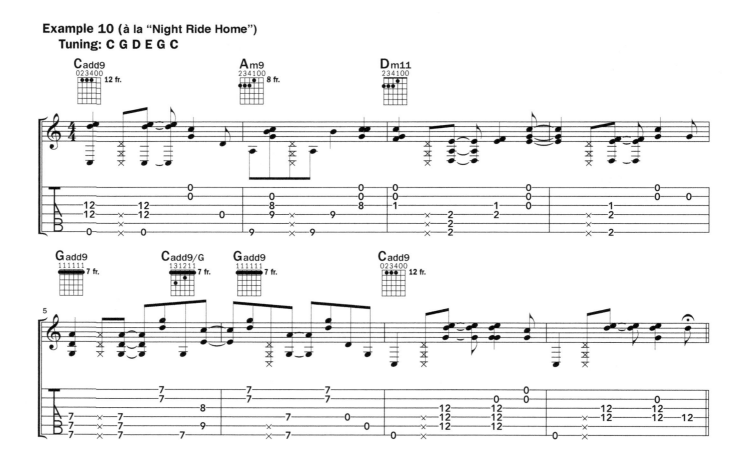

Example 10 (à la "Night Ride Home")
Tuning: C G D E G C

Try a similar groove in **Example 11**, going back and forth between two chord shapes used in "The Magdalene Laundries," the haunting track from *Turbulent Indigo*. The tuning B F B E A E, used on no other Mitchell song, has a huge range, with the sixth string plunging to B and the first at the standard E. Note that this song is not in the key of B, as you might expect, but in A; the I chord is rooted at the tenth fret of the sixth string. In terms of percussion, the main thumb slap is again on beat 2, though throughout her songs Mitchell freely adds syncopated accents, like a jazz drummer.

In considering her rhythmic sense, it's interesting to check out what happened when Mitchell revisited "Big Yellow Taxi" in 2007 for the album *Shine*. Gone was the straight-up folk-rock strumming of the original. Instead she played a syncopated groove similar to **Example 12**, with plenty of string percussion and damping for a staccato feel. You may find, as I did, that using your fingers, rather than a pick, makes it easier to approximate the sound.

Example 11 (à la "The Magdalene Laundries")
Tuning: B F♯ B E A E

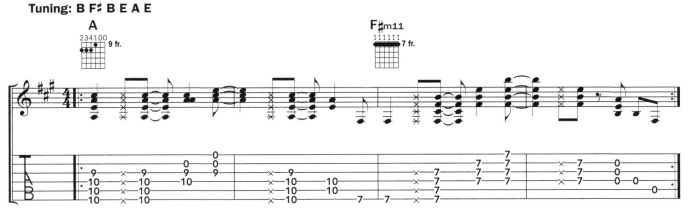

Example 12 (à la "Big Yellow Taxi" 2007)
Tuning: D A D F♯ A D

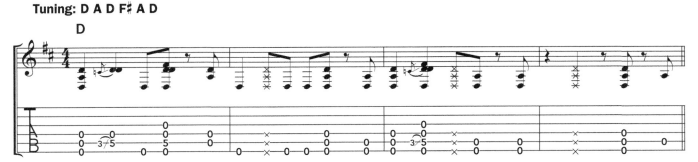

ON THE PATH

Mitchell's approach to guitar no doubt has inspired many players to turn those tuners and search for new ideas by getting lost in alternate tunings. Some contemporary guitarist/songwriters come across as highly influenced by Mitchell—the talented young artist Madison Cunningham is one example I recently encountered. But Mitchell's whole style is so unusual that you'd be hard-pressed to find a true soundalike guitarist. Sue Tierney sees Mitchell in this regard as an outlier: "The only other person I would put in this category," she says, "is Michael Hedges, who took the guitar and made it sound like a completely different instrument."

Blackburn comments, "I do see players like David Wilcox and Jonatha Brooke playing in the Joni-esque hybrid style. But it's not just a technique or 'style,' anyway; it is her whole vision of inventing fresh sonorities and voicings from one song to the next, always in search of an emotional color suitable to the lyrics. James Taylor, Joni's old friend and lover, described her composing as not just painting on a canvas but designing a fresh canvas first—for each song! How many of us have the patience or the doggedness to do that?"

It's poignant to delve into Mitchell's music like this at a time when the artist herself is no longer active. A few years ago, following her near-fatal aneurysm, reports of her health were grim. But Eric Andersen, who remains in close touch with Mitchell—she is the godmother of his daughter, Sari—shares a hopeful image from a recent visit to her home. He sang Mitchell's own classic "River" to her, and the songwriter herself joined in, softly.

"They told us it was the first time she sang since her collapse and recovery," he says. "I put an open-tuning guitar in her lap and she strummed it a while. Very moving to see my sister in action."

TUNINGS BY NUMBER

To wrap your head around Mitchell's tunings, it's helpful to understand her own system (by way of her guitar archivist, Joel Bernstein) for tracking tunings: Name the pitch of the lowest string and then, for the others, the fret number that equals the pitch of the next string. Standard tuning, by this system, is E 5 5 5 4 5: from the low E string to the A string is five frets; from the A string to the D string is five frets; and so on. Open D (D A D F♯ A D) is D 7 5 4 3 5.

This number system is not only handy for getting in tune string by string but shows how the same relative tunings recur at different pitches. Mitchell's tunings lowered over the years along with her voice, so while she started off with open E or open D, for instance, later she favored open C or even open B—all with the same intervals between strings (bass note and then 7 5 4 3 5). Many of her tunings use 7 7 or 7 5 on the low end, with varied intervals on top. You can see how these tuning families work in the well-designed database on jonimitchell.com, and in the tuning tables in the *Complete So Far* songbook.

GEARING UP FOR TUNING DOWN

A deep dive into Mitchell's tunings can be disorienting not only for your fingers but for your guitar. Just ask Dave Blackburn, who with his wife, Robin Adler, has performed six entire Mitchell albums, from *Blue* to *Mingus*. "What really doesn't work is tuning and retuning one guitar from song to song as she valiantly did, without a tuner, in the early club days," he says. "The neck hates the tension changes, and the strings chafe against the nut and saddle and break often, even when tuning lower. What works for me is to set up a few guitars with appropriate string gauges and leave them that way for days or weeks."

For Mitchell tunings in which the bass strings go way down while the trebles are fairly close to standard, you may be well served with a string set like D'Addario's EJ19, with medium-gauge bass strings and lights on top. For tunings that are low across the board, Blackburn recommends setting up an inexpensive baritone acoustic, such as the Alvarez ABT60, with custom gauges that are matched as closely as possible to their intended pitches.

"So, for example, for songs that are in the C G D E G C tuning, I'll put a .059 or .065 on the bottom, an A string dropped to G for the fifth, a regular D on the fourth, a very light D tuned up to E for the third, a wound G for the second, and a B string tuned up to C for the first," he says. "It intonates perfectly, as all the strings are close to their normal tension, and the scale of the baritone helps the deep strings resonate."

TWO GUITARS ARE BETTER THAN ONE

If you spend time trying to learn Mitchell's precise guitar parts off the records, you'll soon discover one complication: Often there are two or more guitars playing similar but not exactly the same parts. Even early songs like "The Circle Game" have double-tracked guitars. The effect was particularly pronounced on *Hejira*, where the guitar parts were looser. On a song like "Hejira," says Howard Wright, "the way the doubled guitars create accidental—or perhaps deliberate—small variations, there's a beautiful blurring and softening effect." Mitchell carried the multitracking approach to its extreme on *Chalk Mark in a Rainstorm*, overlaying 20-some guitar tracks in songs like "My Secret Place."

Since it isn't possible to recreate the multi-tracked sound precisely using one guitar, once you get the shapes down, focus on the overall feel rather than following an exact pattern. That's true to the way Mitchell did it, too. **AG**

Trigger Fingers

Willie Nelson Channels Django Reinhardt's Spirit

By Adam Levy

This feature originally appeared in the July 2018 issue of Acoustic Guitar *magazine.*

Legend has it that singer/songwriter Willie Nelson loves his tour bus so much that he prefers to sleep aboard it—parked outside his home—even when he's not touring. True or not, the story is believable. After many thousands of nights on the road, a bunk is bound to feel more comforting than any bed. Nelson has been touring relentlessly as long as anyone can remember. Unlike most artists, who'll hit the road primarily to promote a new release, Nelson just keeps on keeping on, whether or not he has a new album to plug.

At any given moment, however, odds are good that Nelson does have a new record out. Since beginning his recording career in the early 1960s, he has released more than 70 studio albums, two dozen collaborative albums, several live recordings, and countless compilations. His latest studio effort, *Last Man Standing*, was released on April 27, 2018—two days before his 85th birthday.

Many of Nelson's original songs are now classics of the country canon—including "Crazy," "Bloody Mary Morning," "On the Road Again," "Funny How Time Slips Away," "Night Life," and "Three Days." Despite his popularity as an artist, he was a behind-the-scenes songwriter first. Consequently, the best-known versions of many Nelson songs are by other recording artists. "Crazy" is most often associated with vocalist Patsy Cline. "Night Life" was a hit for Ray Price, and many blues fans are familiar with B.B. King's version. "Three Days" was a 1962 hit for Faron Young and did well for k.d. lang in 1990.

Nelson is almost never seen or heard without his well-worn nylon-string guitar, Trigger (named after film cowboy Roy Rogers' horse), in hand. He acquired this Martin N-20 in 1969. He'd previously been playing a Baldwin nylon-string model, equipped with that company's proprietary Prismatone pickup, played through a solid-state Baldwin C1 amplifier. That guitar got busted up by a drunken patron's misstep while Nelson was gigging on the outskirts of San Antonio, Texas. When Nelson sent the Baldwin guitar back home to Nashville to be revived, the repairman told him it was beyond hope, and mentioned that he had a new Martin for sale. Since Nelson had liked the Baldwin's amplified tone, he asked the repairman to pull the pickup from his totaled guitar and install it in the Martin, and Trigger was born. Nelson has been playing Trigger ever since, and the guitar and amp setup is as much a part of his musical persona as his voice is.

A JAZZ INSPIRATION

Though Nelson is most easily described as a country musician, elements of jazz have always permeated his style. This may be most apparent on his 1978 album, *Stardust*, on which he croons his way through well-loved jazz standards, such as "Georgia on My Mind" and the album's title track. But even on other albums, when he's playing one of his own three- or four-chord songs, Nelson always takes melodic and harmonic chances. Country may be his milieu but jazz is his M.O.

It's no secret that Nelson's primary inspiration—on the guitar, at least—is the late Gypsy-jazz luminary Django Reinhardt. Echoes of Reinhardt's sinuous melody lines can frequently be heard in Nelson's guitar solos, as you'll see later in this lesson. The first two examples here highlight Nelson's notable rhythm-guitar style, which exhibits some Gypsy-jazz sophistication, as well.

Example 1 is based on Nelson's recording of "I'm Falling in Love Again" from his 1992 album *The IRS Tapes: Who'll Buy My Memories?* (Long story short: Nelson owed back taxes. To satisfy his debt, he negotiated a deal to record and release this music and give the proceeds to the taxman.) The lush passing chords in measures 1 and 2 aren't typical country fare but are Nelsonic indeed. D♭9/A serves as a chromatic approach to C9/G. G♭6 functions similarly, approaching the F chord—though without the parallel voicing motion. Interestingly, the remainder of this passage is purely triadic. Nelson has never seemed to mind mixing jazz flavors with campfire sensibilities.

Example 1 (à la "I'm Falling in Love Again")

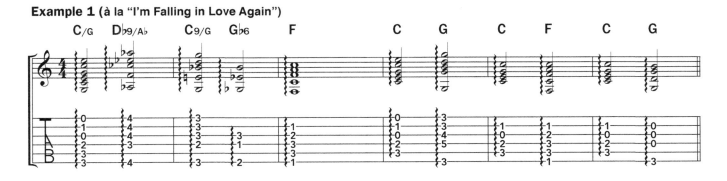

If you want to dig deep into Nelson's guitar style, *The IRS Tapes* is a great place to start because it was recorded without any additional production or orchestration. It's just his voice and guitar throughout, presumably tracked live in the studio.

COLORING OUTSIDE THE LINES

VH1 Storytellers: Johnny Cash & Willie Nelson is another great opportunity to hear Nelson's guitar in the foreground. Recorded at a live concert appearance in 1997 (and released a year later), the album features just these two, singing some of their best-loved songs. They both play guitar, and take alternate turns on lead vocal. **Example 2** is composite—inspired by Nelson's freewheeling fills and Cash's rock-steady rhythm on their version of "Funny How Time Slips Away" from *VH1 Storytellers*.

The first three measures are straightforward—à la Cash—except for the Ab on beat 4 of measure 1. That's pure Nelson. (Going to a G chord? Why not get there by half step?) Measure 4 incorporates a rootless A9 arpeggio, starting on the chord's third (C#). Played smoothly—as Nelson would—the maneuver sounds much more complex than it is.

Example 2 (à la "Funny How Time Slips Away")

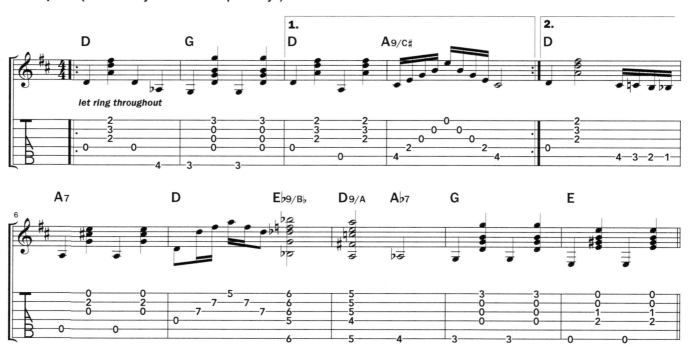

Example 3a is in the style of Nelson's intro to "Are You Sure," from his mid-'60s album *Country Willie—His Own Songs*. Trigger wasn't in his hands just yet but he'd already been developing a singular voice on the guitar. This example illustrates Nelson's uncanny ability to keep the fundamentals covered while coloring outside the lines. You can see how the new chords are outlined fairly clearly at the beginning of each measure, yet there's some sly chromaticism to be found in between.

In **Example 3b**—also styled after "Are You Sure"—the fills get bluer and richer, harmonically speaking. Check out the two-note shapes in measure 2 and three-note shapes in measure 5. As before, these aren't difficult grabs, but they can sound incredibly cool when you play them with confidence. The rest of the fills here are common blues vocabulary, paced to complement Nelson's vocal delivery. Make sure to listen to the original recording.

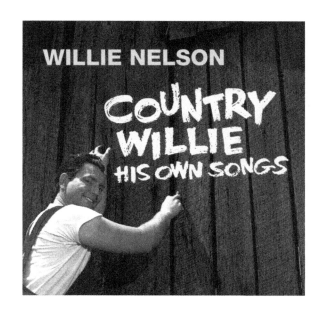

Example 3a (à la "Are You Sure")

Example 3b

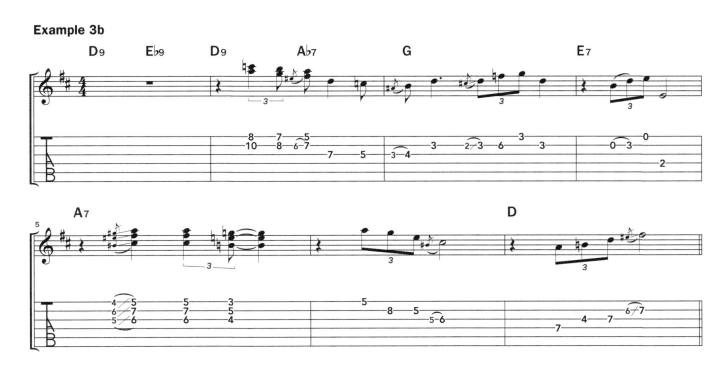

"Darkness on the Face of the Earth" is another song from *Country Willie* that showcases Nelson's guitar skills. **Example 4** is in the style of the song's introduction. Guitarists don't always think of the key of F major as one that can feature hammer-ons from open strings. This example illustrates that there are plenty of melodic possibilities.

CHROMATIC ANTICS

Nelson had previously recorded "Darkness on the Face of the Earth" on his 1962 debut album, *And Then I Wrote*, and he revisited it once again on his 1998 album, *Teatro*. His guitar work on this later recording is completely different, though no less inventive. The next two examples are inspired by Nelson's thrilling mid-song solo. **Example 5a** begins simply and spaciously, which serves to heighten the drama that follows. In measure 3, an eighth-note line climbs up the E major scale from its sixth degree (C#).

This line changes direction at the end of the measure, morphing into a melodic pattern that continues downward through the first two beats of measure 4. Beats 3 and

4 here are a tumbling blur with chromatic passing tones. A few fingerings may work for this passage, but try this one first: Play the triplet with fingers 3-2-1, then quickly shift down one fret so that your second finger is on F#; finger the 16ths 2-3-2-1, then quickly shift down one more fret so that your first finger is on E for the downbeat of the following measure.

Example 5b is more laid back than Ex. 5a, though tension begins to build in measure 3 as the paired notes descend chromatically. The descending flurry on beat 3 of the fourth measure looks thorny on paper but it's really not. Play the first four notes of the quintuplet with your first finger. Slide from fret 5 to fret 2, then pull off to the open B. Note that on beat 4 of that same bar, the note C# anticipates the A chord in the final measure. (C# is the third of an A major triad.)

Example 4 (à la "Darkness on the Face of the Earth")

Example 5a (à la "Darkness on the Face of the Earth" 1998)

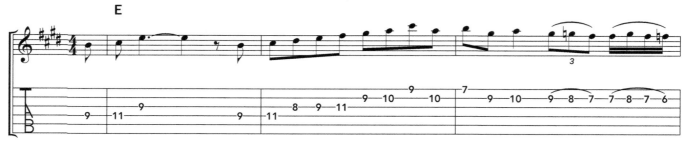

This next example is in the spirit of Nelson's solo on "Angel Flying Too Close to the Ground," a tear-jerking ballad from the soundtrack of the 1981 film *Honeysuckle Rose*, which Nelson also acted in. The song's tempo is slow. Trigger—like most nylon-string guitars—isn't big on sustain. One way Nelson kept his original solo afloat was by re-attacking the notes, very much like you'll see in **Example 6**.

Nelson's other effective tactic was the use of chromatic slurs like those in measures 6 and 8. These moves aren't a far cry from the slurs in Ex. 5b. The difference this time is that the slurs are single notes—not double-stops—and are in the guitar's lowermost register.

Example 5b

Example 6 (à la "Angel Flying Too Close to Home")

Nelson's beautiful "Moonlight in Vermont"—from his '78 album, *Stardust*—is the inspiration for **Example 7**. Play it fingerstyle to best capture the gentle murmur of Nelson's original recording. The chord shapes in measure 1 will likely be familiar to you, though the shapes in measure 2 may not if you haven't played much jazz. Note that this Fmaj7 voicing has no third (A) in it but sounds complete nonetheless—perhaps because the note A is played in the previous measure and seems to linger. Gaug7 is a G7 chord with a raised fifth degree (D♯). The B♭7 chord in measure 4 is a familiar first-fret barre chord, though its sound is surprising in this key, as the song's composer, Hoagy Carmichael, intended. Remember—this example is merely the song's brief introduction. If the final G chord feels unresolved to you, play a C chord afterward. AG

Example 7 (à la "Moonlight in Vermont")

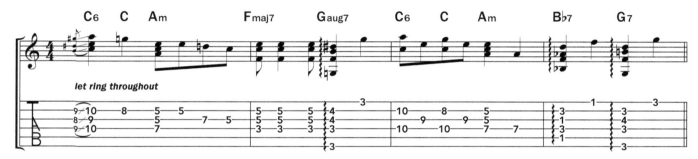

CAROL M. HIGHSMITH, LIBRARY OF CONGRESS PHOTO

SCOTT NEWTON

American Icon

Exploring the Late John Prine's Simple but Distinctive Guitar Work

By Jeffrey Pepper Rodgers

At any given song circle, open mic, or other gathering of guitar pickers and singers, it usually won't be long until someone breaks into a John Prine song. From "Paradise" to "Angel from Montgomery" to "In Spite of Ourselves," Prine's songs are essential repertoire in the country/folk/Americana songbook, because they are both accessible and unforgettable. With the simplest ingredients—a handful of chords, a roughhewn voice with limited range—Prine created evocative stories-in-song that could be poignant, profound, and funny as hell.

Prine's place in the pantheon of American songwriting became clear when the hard news hit in April that he'd passed away, at 73, due to complications from the coronavirus. His health had long been poor, as he endured multiple bouts with cancer, but Prine had delivered the warm and wise album *The Tree of Forgiveness* in 2018—the highest-charting release of his career—followed by triumphant touring, and it seemed like his music would keep coming. In the weeks following his death, tributes poured in from generations of artists: Bonnie Raitt, Roger Waters, Jason Isbell, Sturgill Simpson, Brandi Carlile, Dave Matthews, Jeff Tweedy, Kacey Musgraves, and on and on. The words that stuck with me most came from country/folk singer-songwriter Iris DeMent, Prine's longtime friend and frequent collaborator.

"John Prine was, without a doubt, one of the greatest songwriters this world will ever know," DeMent wrote on Facebook. "Here's why he rests on my heart's mountaintop: Because he cared enough to look—at me, you, all of us—until he saw what was noble, and then he wrapped us up in melodies and sung us back to ourselves. That was the miracle of John Prine. And it was enough."

Prine was known most of all for his lyrical gifts, but the foundation of all his music was his flattop guitar, which he strummed and fingerpicked with a few classic styles that provided everything he needed to accompany a lifetime of songs. This lesson takes a tour of Prine's music by way of his guitar style, using examples drawn from some of his most-loved songs. As with every aspect of his music, Prine managed to make simple guitar patterns distinctive. Even without the melody and words, the guitar parts sound like songs.

This feature originally appeared in the November/December 2020 issue of Acoustic Guitar *magazine.*

THE SINGING MAILMAN DELIVERS

In 1970, journalist Roger Ebert happened to walk into a Chicago folk club called the Fifth Peg and caught a set by Prine, who had only started performing the year before and worked by day as a mail carrier. Ebert was astounded to hear the young, unassuming singer deliver songs like. "Angel from Montgomery" and "Hello in There," and he wrote a full-page review for the *Chicago Sun-Times* under the headline "Singing Mailman Who Delivers a Powerful Message in a Few Words."

Ebert quoted the devastating chorus of "Sam Stone," Prine's portrait of a drug-addicted veteran: "There's a hole in Daddy's arm where all the money goes." Ebert wrote, "You hear lyrics like these, perfectly fitted to Prine's quietly confident style and his ghost of a Kentucky accent, and you wonder how anyone could have so much empathy and still be looking forward to his 24th birthday." Anyone spinning Prine's self-titled debut from the following year would have to wonder the same thing—how could any songwriter deliver songs with such depth, maturity, and emotional range seemingly right out of the gate?

Prine was steeped in early country music, from the Carter Family to Hank Williams, and had learned old-time styles through his older brother. In "Paradise," one of the many gems from his debut album, Prine so successfully tapped into traditional sounds that even bluegrass patriarch Bill Monroe initially mistook it for a song from the '20s. In 1967, when Prine was in the Army, he received a letter from his father with a newspaper clipping about how his childhood home of Paradise, Kentucky, had been bought, strip-mined, and torn down by the coal company. So Prine wrote "Paradise" for his father. "First of all, I wanted to put him in the song, because I knew he'd like the song if he was in it," Prine said in 2019 while introducing "Paradise" at the Country Music Hall of Fame and Museum. "And the second reason is, I wanted him to know I was a songwriter."

John Fogerty, one of the scores of artists who've covered "Paradise," told me in a 2009 *AG* interview that Prine's song is "a touchstone for people like us who becry the way corporations get to run roughshod over what may be desired by the little guy, but he's powerless to stop it or stand in the way."

"Paradise" is a straight-up three-chord waltz. Prine used a simple bass/strum pattern in the key of D, as shown in **Example 1**. Play bass notes on beat one and strums on beats two and three, with a few connecting bass runs and a quick hammer-on (measure 6) for variety.

Example 1 (à la "Paradise")

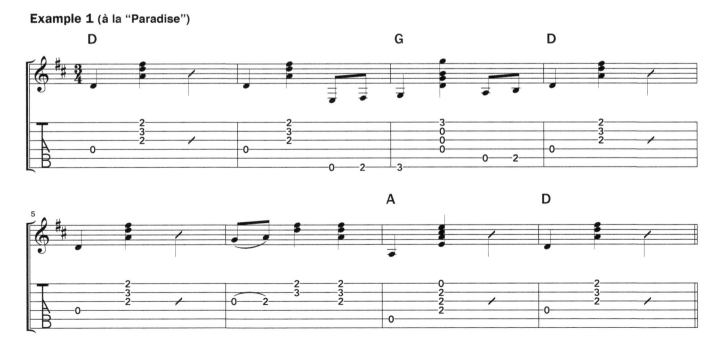

SKETCHING CHARACTERS

The next example is based on another enduring song from Prine's debut, "Hello in There," a portrait of a lonely older couple who've grown disconnected from their kids and each other. In a moving tribute after Prine's death, Brandi Carlile covered "Hello in There" and noted its relevance to vulnerable people living in isolation during the pandemic—as the song asks us not to pass by people with "hollow ancient eyes," but to acknowledge and greet them.

"Hello in There" has far more chords than the usual Prine song. In **Example 2**, play fingerstyle (Prine typically used a thumbpick and his bare fingers), with an alternating bass and a melody on top—a style that goes back to Prine's beginnings as a guitarist. "I learned how to fingerpick by trying to pick like Elizabeth Cotten and Mississippi John Hurt," he told *Fresh Air*'s Terry Gross in 2018. "When I was 14 years old, I'd sit in the closet in the dark, in case I ever went blind, to see if I could play."

Use a capo at the fifth fret and play a steady alternating bass throughout with your thumb. Pick the high strings mostly on the off beats. Add hammer-ons in measures 2, 8, and 12. Prine often used his thumb for fretting sixth-string notes under chords like G, D/F♯, and F, but this example is also playable without thumb fretting.

"Souvenirs," from Prine's second album, *Diamonds in the Rough*, is another early song that reveals an old soul. In just a few words, Prine evoked the burdens of nostalgia. "Broken hearts and dirty windows make life difficult to see," he sang. "That's why last night and this morning always look the same to me."

Prine often performed "Souvenirs" with fellow Chicago songsmith Steve Goodman, and the version on *Diamonds in the Rough*

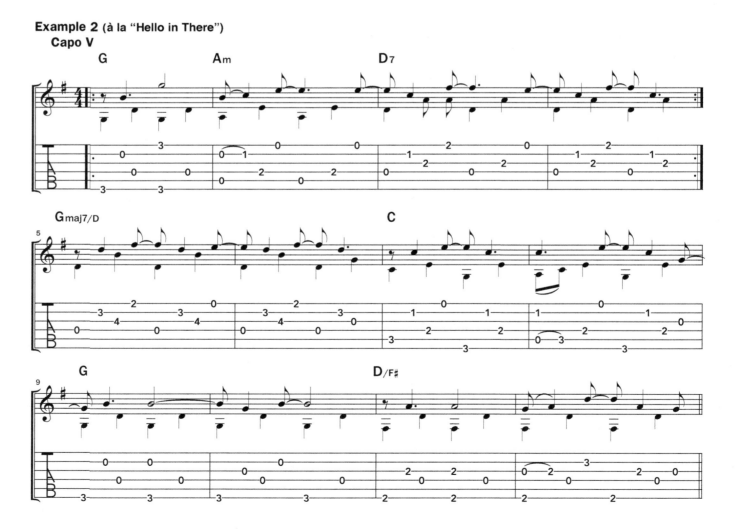

Example 2 (à la "Hello in There")
Capo V

entwines their two guitars—Prine playing D shapes at capo five, Goodman using C shapes at capo seven—and also has them trading off lead vocals. (On the later *Souvenirs* album, released in 2000, Prine dropped the key and capoed at the second fret.) As in many of his songs, Prine picked the melody instrumentally before entering with the vocal, playing a part similar to **Example 3**. In measure 3, lower the bass a half step under the G, to F♯, before going to the A7. Again, Prine would fret these bass notes with his thumb.

Example 3 (à la "Souvenirs")
Capo V

Example 4 (à la "Dear Abby")
Capo IV

THE LIGHT SIDE

For a songwriter whose lyrics could be so sad, Prine was a master of sly comic writing, with songs like the cheerfully morbid "Please Don't Bury Me," the silly/flirty "Let's Talk Dirty in Hawaiian," and "Dear Abby," the advice column in song with the useful reminder that "you are what you are, and you ain't what you ain't."

Example 4 shows the style Prine used to accompany "Dear Abby," released as a live track on the 1973 album *Sweet Revenge*. Like "Paradise," "Dear Abby" is a flatpicked waltz, played uptempo using G shapes. Capo on the fourth fret to match Prine's key of B major, and use quick, light down-up strums for the pairs of chords as in measures 1, 4, 5, and so on.

At the end of the '90s, Prine came back from a battle with cancer with *In Spite of Ourselves*, an album of classic country duets with Emmylou Harris, Lucinda Williams, Trisha Yearwood, Patty Loveless, and others. The title track was the album's sole original, with endearing, mildly risqué banter between Prine and Iris DeMent.

"*In Spite of Ourselves*," DeMent told me in a 2012 *AG* interview, "was a big hurdle for me. John had just survived cancer and decided he wanted to go back in the studio. I think that's one of the first songs he recorded and he asked me to do it, and I said yes before I saw the lyrics…. It's kind of funny, talking about that song now, because I've sang it a thousand times with him all over the country and I feel completely comfortable and it's fun and playful. But when I heard it the first time it was a little bit like…'I've got to make sure my mom never hears this.' That seems silly now."

The guitar part for "In Spite of Ourselves" is another example of Prine's melodic fingerpicking in the style of "Freight Train." In **Example 5,** play out of C shapes, with the melody on the top strings. Keep up the alternating bass except for in measures 2, 4, and 8, where you stay put on the C bass note for three beats.

Example 5 (à la "In Spite of Ourselves")

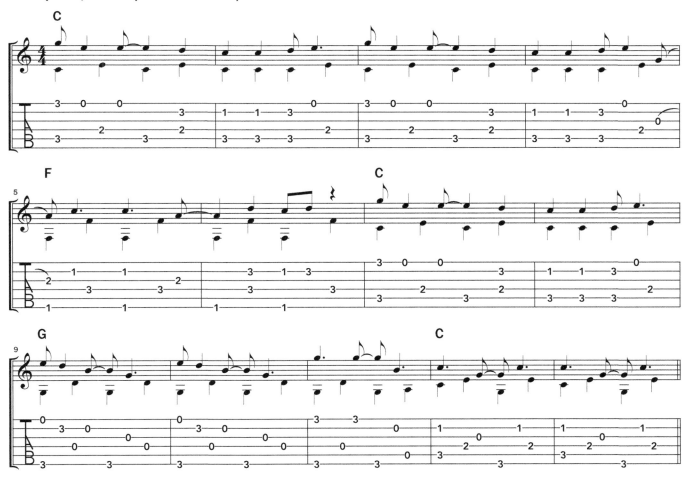

LAST CHORUS

Prine's 2018 album, *The Tree of Forgiveness*, was in many ways the perfect parting word—it even closed with his musings on the afterlife in "When I Get to Heaven." (One posthumous song was released in June: the equally appropriate farewell "I Remember Everything.") *The Tree of Forgiveness* featured a number of co-writes (including one, oddly enough, with Phil Spector) and support from Jason Isbell, Amanda Shires, and Brandi Carlile.

One track that has been widely adopted by other artists—and Prine's own favorite from the album—is "Summer's End," which Prine wrote with his longtime collaborator Pat McLaughlin. Among the many covers to be found online are lovely versions by Phoebe Bridgers (on guitar) and Sierra Hull (on octave mandolin). Over a wistful melody, "Summer's End" shows Prine's knack for finding just the right image to convey an emotional landscape:

You never know how far from home you're feeling
Until you watch the shadows cross the ceiling
Well, I don't know but I can see it snowing
In your car the windows are wide open

"Summer's End" is fingerpicked with C shapes and a capo on the second fret, causing it to sound in the key of D major. During the verse, Prine plays a pattern similar to **Example 6**. Hammer onto the second string for the C chord in measures 1 and 2, then shift to E minor; the first four measures serve also as an intro/interlude. Then move to an F and G for the remainder of the example, maintaining the alternating bass throughout.

THE SONG GOES ROUND

In April, New Orleans–based songwriter Carsie Blanton—one of countless musicians mourning the loss of Prine—responded in pitch-perfect fashion with the two-minute ditty "Fishin' with You," which borrows its melody from Prine's song "That's the Way the World Goes Round" and some chord voicings from "Fish and Whistle." In lyrics that quote a bunch of other Prine songs ("Crazy as a Loon," "Paradise," "It's a Big Old Goofy World," "Spanish Pipedream"), she thanks him for the tunes and the way he "made us all wanna sing." After a quick selfie video of "Fishin' with You" circulated widely on social media, Blanton released a single with contributions from, among others, Oliver Wood and Sara Watkins with all proceeds going to charities named by Prine's family.

"I have loved John's songs all my life," Blanton said when I asked what she'd learned about songwriting from Prine's example. "He taught me how to be vulnerable and sweet, and how to temper that with humor so it doesn't cause a toothache." AG

Example 6 (à la "Summer's End")
Capo II

Moods & Melodies

Inside Paul Simon's Atmospheric Acoustic Guitar Style

By Adam Levy

Whether you think of Paul Simon as the guitar-playing, songwriting half of the duo Simon & Garfunkel or as a solo artist with world-music leanings may depend on your age. Both characterizations are true—if vastly oversimplified. Simon is a songwriter and guitarist who has made many iconic records—with Art Garfunkel and without—and has composed some of the most beloved songs of the 20th century. Along the way, he's experimented with all sorts of musical styles and recording techniques—and guitars.

Simon is known to be particular about the instruments he plays and is a bit of a six-string connoisseur. When the Metropolitan Museum of Art presented the exhibit Guitar Heroes: Legendary Craftsmen from Italy to New York, in 2011, Simon lent his 1975 D'Aquisto New Yorker Special oval-hole archtop to display. He has played several Martin models over the years—including a D-12-28,

D-35S, and his OM-42PS signature model. He has also favored an early 1970s SB3 built by luthier Michael Gurian, as well as assorted Guilds and Yamahas.

What's been consistent throughout Simon's long career is that he's always pushed himself to explore the guitar beyond typical folk and folk-rock styles. "So Long, Frank Lloyd Wright" (from Simon & Garfunkel's 1970 album, *Bridge Over Troubled Water*) bears an obvious bossa-nova influence. "Something So Right" (from Simon's 1973 solo record, *There Goes Rhymin' Simon*) is peppered with jazz-tinged passing chords. "American Tune" (from the same album) was partially inspired by a J. S. Bach melody. Simon explored South African musical styles on his 1986 *Graceland* album and Brazilian and Cameroonian rhythms on *Rhythm of the Saints* (1990). On the albums that followed—including *You're the One* and *Surprise*—Simon continued to use rhythm as a prime source of inspiration.

Simon's latest album—*Into the Blue Light*, released last September—features new recordings of ten songs spanning his solo career. Each song's arrangement has been completely overhauled. Many are orchestrated with no guitar at all, or with guitars played by other fine players—including Sérgio and Odair Assad, Bill Frisell, Mark Stewart, and the late Cameroonian guitarist Vincent Nguini, who worked with Simon beginning in the late '80s. Simon recently announced his retirement from touring, so his summer 2018 outing—Homeward Bound: The Farewell Tour—was (supposedly) his last. It remains to be seen whether he will continue to record.

In this lesson, you'll study a trove of examples inspired by Simon's sophisticated, evocative acoustic-guitar work—with Garfunkel and on his own.

DEFT FINGERPICKING AND CREATIVE CHORDING

Example 1 is in the style of the intro section to "Kathy's Song" from Simon & Garfunkel's *Sounds of Silence*, released at the beginning of 1966. (A solo performance of this song appeared on Simon's 1965 debut, *The Paul Simon Songbook*. The *Sounds of Silence* recording is the reference point here.) To match the recording, tune each of your strings down a half step.

Though this song is in the key of G major, the moody opening measures suggest a darker atmosphere via an incomplete Em(add9) chord. As with all of the examples in this lesson, play the down-stemmed notes with your thumb and the up-stemmed notes with your fingers. While the first four measures are simple enough, there's a move in bars 5 and 7 that requires some extra attention to get just right—because your hands will be moving somewhat independently. After hammering into the C/G chord on the and of beat 2, pluck the lone C note on the and of beat 3 and the E on beat 4. Finally, pull off both strings 2 and 4 on the and of beat 4. That last bit is the tricky part, as you're essentially plucking just one note (the E) then immediately pulling off two (E and C).

Example 1 (à la "Kathy's Song")
Tune down 1/2 step

The lovely "April Come She Will"—also from *Sounds of Silence*—is another example of Simon's deft fingerpicking and creative chording. **Example 2** is based on the intro to this song. (As with "Kathy's Song," an alternate version of "April Come She Will" appeared on *The Paul Simon Songbook*. *Sounds of Silence* is our benchmark here, as well.) Before playing Ex. 2, return your guitar to standard tuning and place a capo at the first fret.

What's notable in this example is Simon's use of high-position triads on the treble strings in lieu of standard open chords. The G/D chord in measures 1, 3, and 5 is fingered like a familiar D major chord but becomes G/D when played at the seventh fret. Simon gets some melodic variety in measures 2, 4, and 6 by lifting his second finger off of the first string. (The open E turns the chord from G/D to G6/D.) In measure 7, you'll briefly play a D triad at fifth fret, followed by open third and fourth strings. While that third-string note (G) isn't part of a D chord, it's harmonious enough and allows time for a quick shift down to open position for the four measures that follow.

Example 2 (à la "April Come She Will")
Capo I

ENTERING WORLDLY TERRITORY

Following the commercial success of *Sounds of Silence*, Simon & Garfunkel released another LP—*Parsley, Sage, Rosemary, and Thyme*—before the end of 1966. The arpeggiated guitar figure in **Example 3** is similar to the mesmeric opening measures of "Scarborough Fair/Canticle" from *Parsley, Sage, Rosemary, and Thyme*. The song is in the key of E minor. To match the original recording, capo your guitar at the seventh fret and play shapes in the proximity of an Am7 chord—though never land directly on it.

Simon's fingerpicking pattern here is pretty unusual. If you watch some of his live performances of this song on YouTube, you may notice that he doesn't seem to use his middle finger, opting instead for his thumb (for the down-stemmed notes in this example) in conjunction with his index and ring fingers (up-stemmed notes).

Example 3 (à la "Scarborough Fair/Canticle")

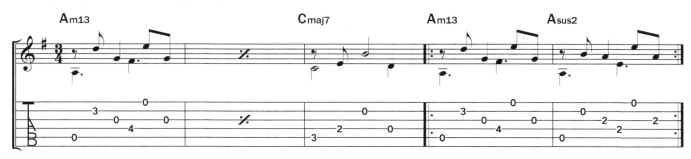

Simon & Garfunkel's final studio recording, *Bridge Over Troubled Water*, was released in 1970. It demonstrates that Simon was moving beyond folk and folk-rock into more adventurous, worldly territory. "El Condor Pasa," for example, is based on a traditional Peruvian song. The album's title track is influenced by gospel music. "So Long, Frank Lloyd Wright," played on nylon-string guitar, has a bossa-nova feel—with undulating rhythms and jazzy chords. **Example 4a** is modeled on the verse sections of that tune. If you'd like to match Simon & Garfunkel's recording, tune down a half step. Note that the guitar part is more melodically active in measures 4, 7, and 8. This is because the vocal melody is relatively inactive in those places. That's a great lesson to remember.

Example 4b echoes the tangy chords Simon plays at the end of the song's second verse—juxtaposing a fretted D against an open E on the C major chord, then similarly playing a fretted A against an open B on the G major chord. Measure 4 has a similar dissonance, though it's achieved in a slightly different way. In measures 1 and 2, the fretted note is the chord's #2, while the open string is the chord's major 3. Here, however, the #2 (B) is open and the 3 (C) is fretted.

Example 4a (à la "So Long, Frank Lloyd Wright")
Tune down 1/2 step

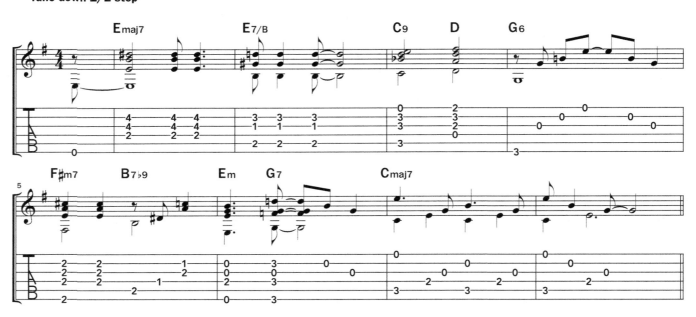

Example 4b

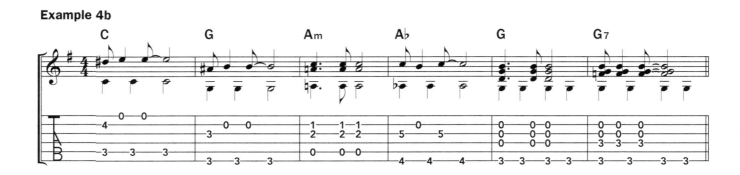

JAZZ-TINGED HARMONIES AND MORE

The remaining examples in this lesson are drawn from Simon's post-S&G career. In these, you'll see how he has continued to grow as a guitarist and as a composer—with the use of even more colorful harmonies and guitar techniques that definitely don't come from the folk-guitar tradition.

The first solo Simon song you'll look at is "Something So Right," from his eclectic 1973 release, *There Goes Rhymin' Simon*. To play **Example 5**, which is in the style of Simon's recorded intro to this song, tune your guitar up a half step. Alternatively, you could capo at the first fret. (It's unknown whether Simon tuned up or used a capo on his original studio recording. When he performed "Something So Right" on *The Paul Simon Special* in 1977, he used no capo, so his nylon-string guitar must've been tuned up. If you can find this performance on YouTube, or elsewhere, it's a worthwhile watch.)

In measure 1, the chord shape is transformed from Esus4 to Emaj7, simply by moving the fretted notes down one fret each. Try playing these note pairs with fingers 2 and 4, as Simon apparently does. Use a barre across strings 1 through 4 to efficiently grab the E13sus4 in measure 2, adding your fourth finger for the high C♯. Play the E7 in open position, using your fourth finger for the note D (measure 2, "and" of beat 3). From there, slide the D up to F♯ ("and" of beat 4). Then you'll already have your fourth finger on F♯ in preparation for the A6 in measure 3. Both A6 and A are to be played as full barre chords.

Example 5 (à la "Something So Right")
Tune up 1/2 step

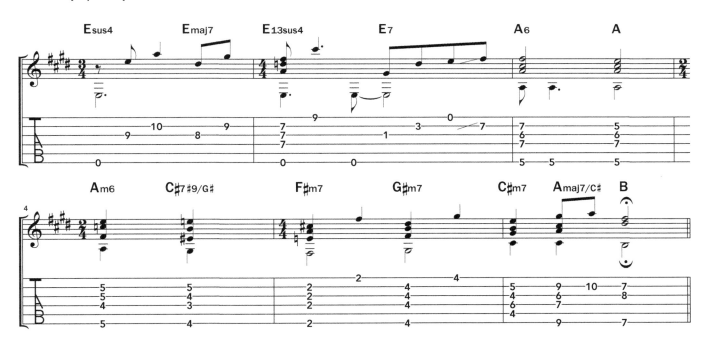

The next two measures are straightforward, technique-wise, though the jazz-tinged harmony is fairly sophisticated. In the final measure, you've got to quickly get your fourth finger from G♯ to A on the and of beat 2. This may take some extra practice if your fourth finger is not particularly agile. The final B chord is played as a full barre.

Example 6a is inspired by the verses of "The Late Great Johnny Ace," a haunting song from Simon's 1983 record *Hearts and Bones*. You've already tuned your guitar up and down by a half step in this lesson. For this song, drop down a whole step from standard tuning. Though the tune is in the key of D major, the first three measures vacillate between B♭maj7 and E—two chords that have little to do with the key of the song, or with each other. The effect of these remote harmonies is appropriately unsettling. (The lyrics of the song reference John Lennon and John F. Kennedy, who were both murdered, as well as the R&B singer Johnny Ace, who accidentally shot himself.)

Though the verses of "The Late Great Johnny Ace" are played freely, with no fixed tempo, the bridge section settles into a steady-rolling shuffle—as seen in **Example 6b**. The trick throughout most of this example is that the bass notes (played with your thumb) are played on offbeats, while the two-note chord shapes land squarely on beats 1–4. If you haven't been tapping your foot in time as you practice these examples, now would be a good time to start! A physical sense of the downbeats may help you keep the chords where they belong, even though the bass is syncopated.

This lesson's final two examples are back in standard tuning and are inspired by the song "Questions for the Angels," from Simon's 2011 release, *So Beautiful or So What*. Though there's no fixed tempo in either example, make sure to keep things moving. This song is meant to lilt.

Example 6a (à la "The Late Great Johnny Ace")
 Tune down 1 step

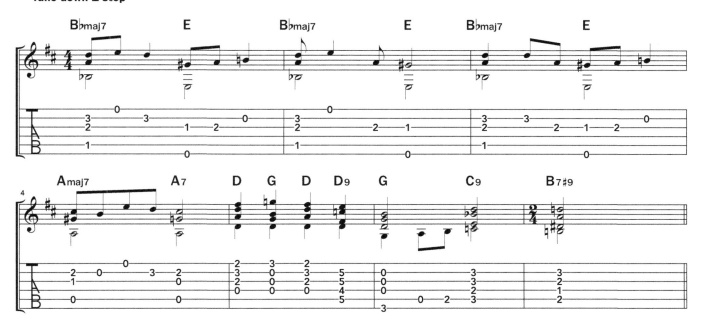

Example 6b

Example **7a** is akin to the song's verses, which employ a Dmaj7 shape rooted on the fifth string at the fifth fret. On the final beat of each of the first four measures, the note B gives the chord more harmonic depth and some melodic energy, as well. **Example 7b** is like the song's chorus. Here, the harmony drifts further from the tonal center (D major) and the meter alternates between 2/4 and 3/4. The effect is dreamy, as is surely Simon's intent. Play the Cm7 (measure 1) as a half-barre across strings 1–4. The rest of this example is in open position. Not all of these chord shapes may be immediately familiar to you, but they're not hard to play.

Now that you've had an opportunity to play some Paul Simon–inspired passages, you should have a greater appreciation of his depth as a composer and as a guitarist. If you simply learn to play these examples note for note, you'll have some intriguing new moves under your fingers. If you're a creative player or writer, it behooves you to develop Simon's ideas further and make them your own. He keeps growing—and you can, too.

Example 7a (à la "Questions for the Angels")

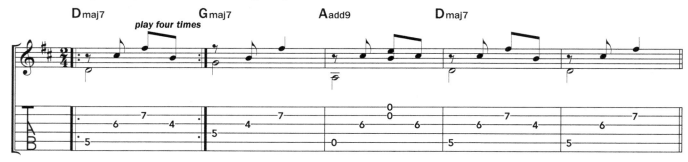

Example 7b

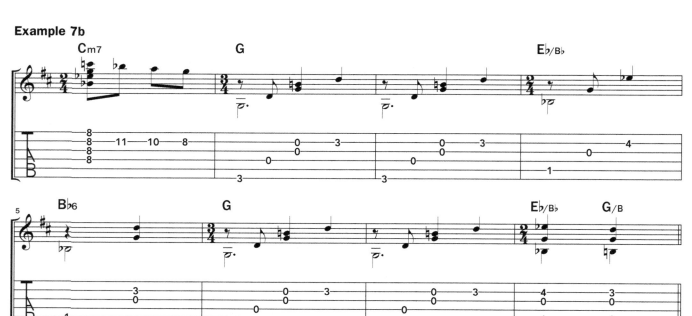

AN UNERRING SENSE OF BALANCE

Longtime sideman Mark Stewart describes his adventures with Paul Simon

Mark Stewart has been central to Paul Simon's recording and touring projects for the past 20 years, adding color and depth with his guitar parts and on several other instruments, as well. In between Simon projects, Stewart keeps busy with all sorts of other interesting endeavors. He teaches instrument design at MIT and plays guitar with the cutting-edge Bang on a Can All-Stars ensemble. He has curated the current Gunnar Schonbeck No Experience Required instrument exhibit at Massachusetts Museum of Contemporary Art and is the artistic director of Guitar Mash, a nonprofit organization that supports music education and communal creativity.   —*Adam Levy*

What are some of the instruments you play onstage with Simon?

A 1967 Fender Telecaster, '67 Gibson ES-335, '68 gold-top Gibson Les Paul, '67 Gibson SG Junior, '65 Danelectro 4021, Bruce Petros acoustic, Fender electric mandolin, Nakamura cello, Conn baritone sax, Maui Xaphoon [a saxophone/recorder hybrid], pennywhistle, and Trombadoo—a slide-didgeridoo instrument that I built. Mine is easily made with two dollars' worth of materials, tops, and has a huge sound. I think it can be heard on *Old Friends: Live on Stage*—concert recordings from Simon & Garfunkel's 2003 reunion tour. I've also used it on a few of Paul's records, doing drones in nifty spots.

Do you have a favorite Simon song to play live?

It's like choosing a favorite food. Impossible to say. So many!

Is there one that's most challenging?

There are different challenges from different time periods of his compositional output. The songs that have a beautiful fragility take special care. "Hearts and Bones" [from Simon's 1983 album of the same name] and "Dazzling Blue" [from Simon's 2011 album, *So Beautiful or So What*] come to mind.

In all the years you've played with Simon, what has struck you most about his musicality?

He is a singular and superb bandleader and arranger, with an unerring sense of balance. As a bandleader, Wynton Marsalis has compared Paul to Duke Ellington. I concur.

The Fresh Ideas of an 'Old Folkie'

How Richard Thompson Has Blended Popular, Folk, and Classical Influences to Stunning Effect

By Mac Randall

The final song of Richard Thompson's 2015 album *Still* is called "Guitar Heroes." Over its seven-and-a-half minutes, the distinguished English singer, songwriter, and guitarist takes on the guise of an aspiring picker, a "bebop twang-headed rock 'n' roll fool" who practices incessantly in an attempt to master the licks of his idols. It's a great excuse for Thompson to ape some of his own favorites: Django Reinhardt, Les Paul, Chuck Berry, James Burton, and the Shadows' Hank Marvin. It's also an acknowledgment of sorts that, to many aficionados, Thompson is himself a hero on the order of those greats, a player of astounding skill and originality—which he proves yet again on the song's closing solo, a feast of twisted runs and hair-raising bends that could be no one else's work.

When Thompson plugs in his Stratocaster, fireworks regularly ensue. But his playing is equally brilliant when he picks up a Martin, Ferrington, Lowden, or any number of others and goes unplugged (and in fact, the crucial rhythm part on "Guitar Heroes" is played on an acoustic, as are the Django and part of the Les Paul sections). Lots of fans would argue that Thompson makes much of his best music when he's by himself, with just an acoustic guitar for company. "I was frequently challenged, and still am, by the idea of adapting things off records to play solo," he told me in a 1994 interview. "If it's something that's been recorded with a band, I think, 'Am I just going to strum, strum, strum like some old folkie, or is there something more interesting I can do? Can I suggest the bass line and lead at the same time?' I try to orchestrate, and sometimes when I do that, I come up with new ideas."

On some level, Thompson could indeed be regarded as an "old folkie." After all, he first came to public attention more than 50 years ago as a founding member of the seminal folk-rock band Fairport Convention. But as we'll see in this lesson, his approach to the acoustic guitar is incredibly eclectic, taking in both the traditional and popular musics of Britain, as well as American country and rock and the classical music of Europe and India. And much of his most innovative playing has sprung, at least in part, from his attempts to transfer music associated with another instrument to the guitar—whether that instrument be piano, accordion, or bagpipes.

This feature originally appeared in the July/August 2019 issue of Acoustic Guitar *magazine.*

INSISTENT ARTICULATIONS AND LUXURIOUS CHORDS

During Thompson's time with Fairport Convention (1967–1970), the band took the unprecedented step of rearranging British folk songs for rock instrumentation. In general, Thompson played lead electric, leaving most acoustic parts to the underrated Simon Nicol, but **Example 1** is inspired by an exception to that rule: Fairport's arrangement of "Nottamun Town," taken from *What We Did on Our Holidays*, the band's second album and first of three to be released in 1969. While Nicol lays down the 6/8 rhythm on this track, Thompson (with his bottom string dropped down to D for extra drone) handles the melody. Note how frequently he hammers on, pulls off, or slides from one note to another, then immediately picks that second note again. This kind of insistent articulation, reminiscent of various wind-instrument techniques, adds bite to the music and is one of his principal stylistic calling cards. The tricky bend in measure 5, meanwhile, is an indication that, even this early in his career, Thompson was already interested in exploring the links between Dublin, Delhi, and Memphis.

After splitting with Fairport, Thompson recorded an excellent solo album, 1972's *Henry the Human Fly*, which was undeservedly panned by the British music press and ignored by consumers. But from this discouraging experience came at least one positive result. Shortly after Henry's release, Thompson married Linda Peters, one of the backing vocalists on the album. Together they formed a new duo, billed simply as Richard and Linda Thompson, and proceeded to make some of the most powerful music ever to emerge from the British folk-rock scene.

Example 1 (à la "Nottamun Town")
Tuning: D A D G B E

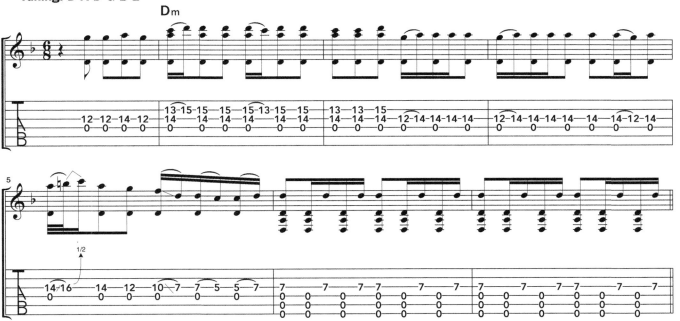

The songs on the couple's first album, 1974's *I Want to See the Bright Lights Tonight*, all of them written by Richard, are as deeply rooted in British folk as Fairport's. Still, some of the most striking moments exhibit an influence of a different sort: French Impressionist composers like Claude Debussy, Maurice Ravel, and Erik Satie. You can hear that in the complex harmony of **Example 2**, based on a sequence from *Bright Lights'* closing track, "The Great Valerio." Two key chords establish a tense, vaguely threatening mood, appropriate for a song about a tightrope walker. Though they are labeled here as Em7♭5/B♭ and G13/A, both are ambiguous, almost diminished chords but not quite. They're also ominous, carrying a sense of foreboding that both the Great Valerio's literal tightrope walk and his observers' figurative one through life are doomed to end in failure. Thompson's debt to Satie in particular is made plain in the song's coda (not seen here), which is a direct lift from "La Balançoire," part of Satie's 1914 cycle of short piano pieces, *Sports et Divertissements*. Note that the guitar is capoed up two frets; Thompson is a frequent capo user, which gives his acoustic playing an extra-crystalline quality.

Example 2 ((à la "The Great Valerio")
Standard tuning, Capo II

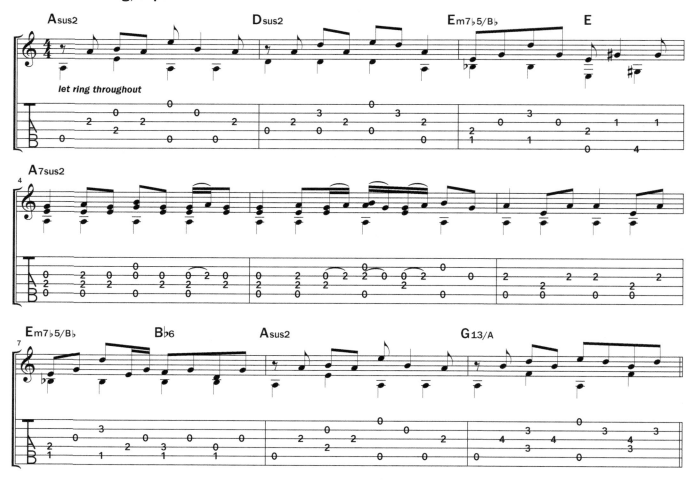

One of Richard and Linda's most enduring ballads, "A Heart Needs a Home," is similarly rich in harmony, but this time the emotional effect is more touching than scary. **Example 3**, drawn from that song, indulges in slow arpeggiations of luxurious chords, beginning with a G6/9 and climaxing on a frankly gorgeous turnaround that implies Cm6 with a major seventh (B) on top. To best capture Thompson's tone, capo your guitar at the fourth fret. The original studio recording of "A Heart Needs a Home," on 1975's *Hokey Pokey*, is lovely, but a live take on the 1993 three-CD Thompson compilation *Watching the Dark* is even better—just two voices, one acoustic guitar, and an enraptured audience.

Example 3 (à la "A Heart Needs a Home")
Standard tuning, Capo IV

AN IMPRESSIVE COMMAND OF THE GUITAR

Example 4 picks up the pace with a reel-like line of the sort that you'd normally expect to hear being played by a fiddle or pennywhistle. The song that inspired it, "Time to Ring Some Changes," was originally recorded by British folk-rock group the Albion Band in 1978, but there's no sign of this chops-challenging part in their rendition. Thompson introduced it when he played the song solo in the early '80s; you can hear his version on the live album *Small Town Romance*, recorded at three U.S. concerts in 1982 and released in 1984. Hammer-ons and pull-offs abound, and although the general vibe is totally olde-England, at least one move in measures 4 and 5—the slide up to D on the fifth string, followed by a ringing open D on the fourth—is straight out of Duane Eddy.

Example 4 (à la "Time to Ring Some Changes")
Tuning: D A D G B E, Capo III

At the time *Small Town Romance* was recorded, Richard and Linda Thompson were in the midst of a messy personal and professional split. Since 1982, Richard has been primarily a solo artist, and his command of the guitar has become an even more essential component of his art. As **Example 5** shows, though, that command isn't always—or even usually—demonstrated through obvious showing-off. This example is based on one of Thompson's prettiest tunes, "Beeswing" from 1994's *Mirror Blue*, and it's proof of how subtle he can be as a player, sketching out a melody and chords but never giving the listener too much information at one time. In measures 7 and 9, notice how a G (open third string) is introduced on what ought to be a standard D chord. This serves two purposes: It craftily anticipates the next chord (a G) and opens up the song's harmony, adding to the overall feeling that something important has been left unresolved.

Example 5 (à la "Beeswing")
Tuning: D A D G B E, Capo III

That lack of resolution is a prime characteristic of certain open tunings, like DADGAD—a Thompson favorite—and the slightly more unusual tuning that anchors what is probably his best-known song, "1952 Vincent Black Lightning," originally released on 1991's *Rumor and Sigh*: C G D G B E (like standard tuning, but with strings 5 and 6 tuned town a whole step each). **Example 6**, which takes

that song as its inspiration, highlights the curious hybrid nature of "Vincent." While the fingers of the picking hand pluck out a line that's akin to Celtic fiddle playing, the thumb sticks mostly to a steady Merle Travis–style root- and fifth boom-chuck, maintaining its rhythm even through the

Example 6 (à la "1952 Vincent Black Lightning")
Tuning: C G D G B E, Capo III

rapid triplet flourishes near the end. On this song and a few others, Thompson often uses a thumbpick in conjunction with his first and second fingers; elsewhere, he favors a regular pick teamed with fingers 2 and 3.

UNUSUAL TWISTS ON CLASSIC IDIOMS

Over the years, fans have come to treasure the ways in which Thompson has recast many of his songs for solo acoustic performance. In the 2010s, he gave a big nod to those fans by recording new all-acoustic versions of 42 selections from his huge back catalog and releasing them on three albums: *Acoustic Classics* (2014), *Acoustic Classics II* (2017), and *Acoustic Rarities* (2017). (See the July/August 2019 issue of *AG* for a transcription of "She Twists the Knife Again," from *Acoustic Classics II*.) These albums make an excellent introduction both to Thompson's songwriting and to his acoustic guitar playing.

Example 7 is based on the *Acoustic Classics II* version of "The Ghost of You Walks." Like "1952 Vincent Black Lightning," it's oriented around a simple root-fifth bass pattern handled by the thumb of the picking hand, only this time the tempo is much more relaxed. And like "The Great Valerio" and "A Heart Needs a Home," it trades in beautiful Debussy-ish harmonic ideas, particularly the Lydian shading of E major over D and the resolution to a D6 chord, which then acquires major-7th and major-9th blossoms thanks to the upper-register melody.

Example 7 (à la "The Ghost of You Walks")
Tuning: D A D G B E, Capo II

Finally, **Example 8**—inspired by "Razor Dance" on 1996's
You? Me? Us?—reveals another key Thompson influence:
Who-style power pop (he's been known to cover the Who's
"Substitute" in concert). The driving rhythm sequence at the
start and 16th-note chord slashes at the end are evidence
of deep drinking from Pete Townshend's well. But you've
got to admit that the bit in-between is from somewhere else
entirely: a tricky, constantly moving bass line shadowed by
a high drone that then mirrors the downward motion of its
low-end companion for just long enough to confuse the fingers on your picking hand. Passages like these make it plain
that, although Thompson's playing can be easily identified,
it can never be pigeonholed.

Example 8 (à la "Razor Dance")
Tuning: D A D G B E, Capo II

RON SLEZNAK

As we noted in the beginning of this piece, Richard Thompson's guitar style incorporates ideas and techniques from a wide range of genres. But interestingly, there's one major genre you won't hear much of in his playing: the blues. And it's not because he doesn't love the work of Robert Johnson or B.B. King. Think back to what was going on in pop, particularly in England, when Fairport Convention first emerged in 1967. London was loaded with guitar heroes—Eric Clapton, Peter Green, Jeff Beck, Jimmy Page—all of them playing music that was largely derived from American blues. How could anyone hope to compete in such a star-heavy marketplace? By sounding different. That's at least part of the reason why Thompson quickly put aside his Gibson Les Paul (a model that the four aforementioned guitarists had all famously played) in favor of a Strat, and why he and Fairport chose to look to the musical history of their own country for inspiration.

"We got to a point," Thompson said in a 2015 interview with *Premier Guitar*, "where we thought, 'We will never play the blues as good as somebody from Chicago.' We'd never been to Chicago—never even to America... If we played music that was more indigenous, music that reflected where we came from, we stood a chance to excel and to be the best in our field."

Five decades and more than 50 albums later, there's little doubt that Thompson has excelled, and that he made a sharp creative choice—one that more would-be artists might benefit from considering. AG

Blue Highways

Inside the Songwriting and Guitar World of Lucinda Williams

By Jeffrey Pepper Rodgers

One of the pivotal moments in the musical life of Lucinda Williams happened long before she started playing guitar. She was around six years old, living in Macon, Georgia, and her father took her downtown to hear a street musician he'd discovered—a blind preacher named Pearly Brown, who sang gospel blues songs with propulsive six- and 12-string guitar and bottleneck slide. "I remember standing there and holding my dad's hand, listening to this guy sing, and just being in utter amazement and bewilderment," Williams recalled. "It was so primal."

Brown's music, heavily indebted to slide master Blind Willie Johnson, was Williams' gateway to the world of country blues. And that music has inspired and guided her ever since, over her more than 40-year career as a singer-songwriter.

Williams is often described as a progenitor of Americana, an artist who blended folk, country, and rock before there was a marketing label for that combo. And she's got the Grammy Awards to prove it: 1993 Best Country Song ("Passionate Kisses"), 1998 Best Contemporary Folk Album (*Car Wheels on a Gravel Road*), and 2001 Best Female Rock Vocal Performance ("Get Right with God"). But blues and gospel run deep in her songwriting, as you can hear throughout her discography, from the gutbucket one-chord blues "Joy"

This feature originally appeared in the September/October 2021 issue of Acoustic Guitar *magazine.*

to the spooky "Pray the Devil Back to Hell" from her latest album, *Good Souls Better Angels*.

At 68, Williams is an icon of American songwriting, an inspiration to several generations of musicians for the way she's married the unvarnished sounds of roots music with a Southern literary sensibility. Through it all, she has developed a sturdy and distinctive rhythm guitar style, usually on a well-traveled Gibson J-45, that supports all of her songs, from brooding ballads to ragged rockers.

In May I connected with Williams by phone from her home in Nashville to learn more about her approach to songwriting and guitar, at what turned out to be strange time for an *Acoustic Guitar* interview. Not long before our conversation, she went public with the news that back in November 2020, she had a major stroke. Though her speaking and singing were unaffected, she was continuing to deal with arm and hand pain and struggling to relearn the guitar essentially from scratch. "I can make the chords, but I can't make my hand move between chords as quickly as it did before," she said. "I feel like when I first took guitar lessons."

Despite this unfortunate context, Williams gamely shared thoughts on her musical inspirations and idiosyncratic guitar style. What follows is a tour of her music by way of some of her best-known songs, with tab examples demonstrating her rhythm playing.

FOLK ROOTS

Williams first got her hands on a guitar—a Silvertone from Sears—when she was 12 and living in Baton Rouge, Louisiana. Her father, the poet and creative writing teacher Miller Williams, found a local rock guitarist to give her lessons, and each week she learned a song, often drawn from the repertoires of '60s folk stars like Joan Baez, Gordon Lightfoot, and Peter, Paul and Mary. Along the way Williams picked up the basics of fingerstyle accompaniment, using a thumbpick and two fingerpicks. "One thing I'm really grateful about was learning those fingerpicking techniques, which I still use today," she said. "I actually don't know how to play with a flatpick."

Albums by Baez and others also introduced Williams to traditional ballads, which she dug into through songbooks like the John and Alan Lomax collection *Folk Song U.S.A.* One favorite trad song, she recalled, was the train-wreck ballad "The FFV" (recorded by the Carter Family as "Engine 143"). No doubt folk ballads helped prepare Williams to tackle tragic stories in her own songs, from the life and death of Texas songwriter Blaze Foley in "Drunken Angel"

to the harrowing account of domestic abuse in "Wakin' Up."

"I really got into the ballads, the English and Irish murder ballads, like 'Banks of the Ohio' and 'Barbara Allen' and all that," she said. "Those are really good lessons in songwriting, 'cause they tell really interesting stories and they're kind of dark and graphic. You know, a guy takes his lover into the woods and stabs her, blood's running down her breast . . . . That stuff was really good to go through and learn."

BLUE NOTES

One of the most impactful discoveries of her early years, as with so many other guitarists of her generation, was Robert Johnson. When a friend in Fayetteville, Arkansas, played her the Columbia album *King of the Delta Blues Singers*, she said, "It just blew me out of the water, you know? I mean, I'd never heard anything like it. It had this dirty, guttural sound, and also his lyrics really got me—it was like blues poetry."

Williams put Johnson front and center when she made her recording debut with *Ramblin' on My Mind* (later shortened to *Ramblin'*), released by Folkways in 1979. Along with several songs she learned from Pearly Brown's record *Georgia Street Singer* ("You're Gonna Need That Pure Religion" and "Motherless Children"), Williams played three Johnson songs, picking a 12-string and doing the songs her way.

The 12-string was a reflection of her earliest public performances. "I was playing out at antiwar demonstrations and all that in the '60s," she said, "and then when I got old enough and traveled to different towns, I was doing a little bit of busking on the streets. The 12-string was good for that, 'cause it was so much louder, and I really liked the sound."

Example 1 shows the kind of rhythm pattern Williams used on "Ramblin' on My Mind." Unlike Johnson, who played slide on "Ramblin'" in an open tuning, Williams played in standard tuning, joined by John Grimaudo on six-string lead. Pick the down-stemmed notes with your thumb and the up-stemmed notes with your index and middle fingers. Williams uses a plastic thumbpick and metal fingerpicks, but you can adapt the basic pattern to however you play.

One of the hallmarks of Williams' style, evident in her earliest tracks, is a strong groove, which she traces to her country blues inspirations as well as electric blues-rock bands like Cream. Early on, she said, "I didn't have a band—that wasn't till much later. So I guess I was improvising and just trying to get a beat thing going without having bass and drums."

To create that kind of drive, strike the bass strings with your thumb or thumbpick force-fully enough to create a percussive slap, and add a little thump on or near the bridge with the heel of your picking hand.

EMERGING AS A SONGWRITER

While her debut showcased Williams as a blues singer, at the same time she was coming into her own as a songwriter. While living in Texas in the '70s, she found a creative home at the storied Houston folk club Anderson Fair, which also nurtured such talents as Nanci Griffith, Lyle Lovett, and Townes Van Zandt.

Example 1 (à la "Ramblin' on My Mind")

Williams introduced herself as a songwriter on the all-original *Happy Woman Blues* in 1980, which—contrary to what the title suggests—leaned mostly away from blues and toward country and especially Cajun sounds, with fiddle-heavy acoustic arrangements. But it wasn't until 1988's *Lucinda Williams*, produced by Gurf Morlix and Dusty Wakeman, that she hit her stride as a singer-songwriter and recording artist, with a core sound built around a combo of acoustic rhythm and electric lead guitars that she has relied on ever since.

Lucinda Williams featured such tracks as the two-chord rocker "Changed the Locks," later covered by Tom Petty, and the song that vaulted her career: "Passionate Kisses," a megahit for Mary Chapin Carpenter. **Example 2** is based on "Side of the Road," another standout from the album in which the narrator walks out into a field, craving a moment of independence, while her lover waits in the car. The image that sparked the song, according to Williams, was the Andrew Wyeth painting "Christina's World"—which depicts a young woman lying in a field gazing toward a farmhouse—coupled with her feeling at the time of being trapped in a relationship and losing her creative spark.

Example 2 (à la "Side of the Road")
Capo IV

"The song is really saying that I want to go back to my life when I felt I was more in control of things and felt more creative," she said. "I'd go through these dry spells with my writing, and that would freak me out."

On the album track, Morlix played electric riffs over Williams' acoustic strumming—she uses a thumbpick like a flatpick. In solo performances, she adds the kinds of simple embellishments shown in the example. The notation shows a single-note picking pattern, but feel free to add adjacent strings while holding down the chord shapes. In songs like this, her right-hand technique is a mix of finger-picking and strumming—akin to banjo frailing.

Williams' collaboration with Morlix continued on 1992's *Sweet Old World* (then fell apart during the making of its follow-up, *Car Wheels on a Gravel Road*). The title track of *Sweet Old World* is one of Williams' best ballads, a meditation on the life experiences lost to suicide. Emmylou Harris, a longtime friend and champion of Williams, beautifully covered the song on her seminal album *Wrecking Ball*.

Williams herself remade the entire *Sweet Old World* album 25 years later and released the results as *This Sweet Old World*, and it's interesting to compare her renditions. **Example 3** is based on her 2017 redo; her acoustic is central, and she plays more slowly and a step lower than in the original—capo 2 rather than 4. (Over the years, she has lowered the capo position in many songs to match her voice.)

The example follows the first part of the verse progression. Play the C chords with a sixth-string G in the bass—her typical voicing for a C—and use an F/C, as well. Often she strums the low strings together rather than playing single bass notes. At the end of measure 2, lift up the F shape and play the open second and third strings—this anticipates the G chord and also gives you a moment to change shapes. You'll find similar transitions in Example 5.

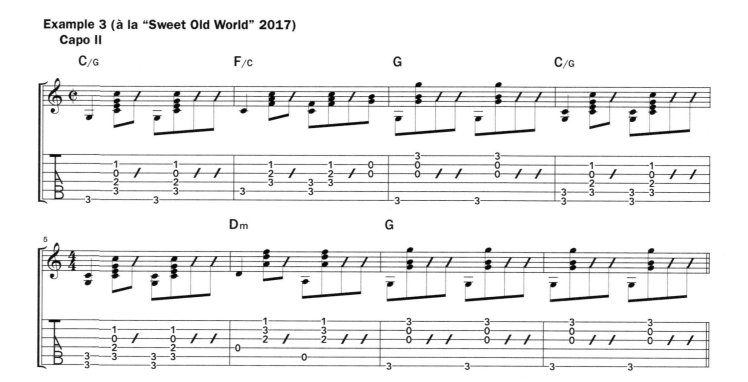

Example 3 (à la "Sweet Old World" 2017)
Capo II

ON THE ROAD

For fans and critics alike, a high point of Williams' career is the Grammy-winning *Car Wheels on a Gravel Road*, from 1998, which last year cracked the top 100 in *Rolling Stone*'s list of the 500 greatest albums of all time. The process of making *Car Wheels* was notoriously long and convoluted (first tracked in Austin with Morlix, redone from scratch in Nashville with Ray Kennedy and Steve Earle, and finally completed in Los Angeles with Ray Bittan of Bruce Springsteen's E Street Band), but the resulting tracks feel vital and visceral.

In the title track, Williams evokes images of her Southern childhood—though she was unaware she was writing from her own experience until her father later pointed it out. Williams often doesn't know what she's tapping into when she writes. "I hate to sound like a cliché, but sometimes I feel like I'm a vehicle for the song coming through," she said. "I just go into that place, let it flow out, and write it down, and then I'll go back and edit—kind of fix it and turn it into something."

Example 4 is based on the flatpick-style intro for "Car Wheels." Toggle between D and Am shapes (capo 4), with some hammer-on embellishments, before landing on the I chord (G). In "Jackson," another highlight of the *Car Wheels* album, she evokes the simplicity and directness of the folk songs she grew up on (and also tips her hat to the song with the same title made famous by Johnny Cash and June Carter). "Sometimes we have to get out of our own way as songwriters," she said. "Sometimes I'll think about the early folk songs and country songs and how simple they were in their chord structure and everything. I have to remind myself that it doesn't have to be real complex. I try to imagine, 'What would Woody Guthrie do?' and put myself back in that place."

Example 4 (à la "Car Wheels on a Gravel Road")
Capo IV

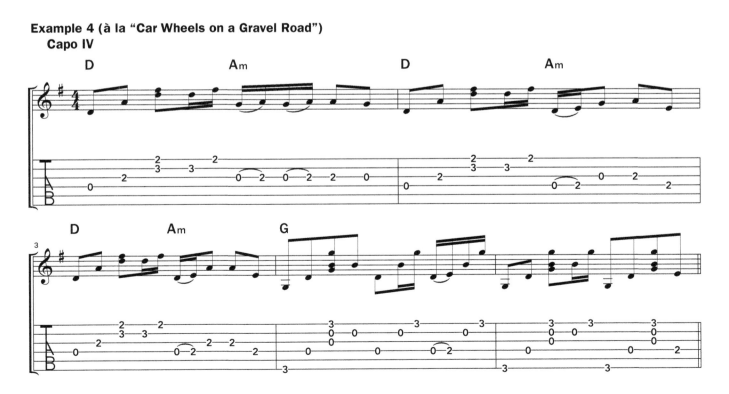

Williams says she didn't play the fingerpicking part on "Jackson" on Car Wheels (she thinks it was Morlix or Earle). Instead, **Example 5** shows the type of pattern she uses live—a thumb/brush, with a bit of chord melody, reminiscent of the Maybelle Carter style. Capo at the third fret to play in the album key.

Example 5 (à la "Jackson")
Capo III

LEAD LINES

Throughout her music, Williams has partnered with top-notch lead guitarists who've helped shape her sound, including Morlix, Doug Pettibone, and, currently, Stuart Mathis. All have added signature riffs that became inseparable from her songs—as with Morlix's jangly riff on "Passionate Kisses."

"After I've written the song, generally the process is I'll do an acoustic demo with just me and guitar, and then I'll send that to the guys in the band and let them listen to it for a while and soak it up," she said. "When we go in the studio, I just let them do what whatever comes to them. I don't ever tell them, 'Play these notes' or anything."

Example 6 shows the riff played by Pettibone that opens and anchors "Fruits of My Labor," released in 2003 on *World Without Tears*. Languid and haunting, the song is back in the spotlight this year thanks to a cover by the indie band Waxahatchee.

On *World Without Tears*, Williams strums "Fruits of My Labor" with a capo at the first fret, and Pettibone plays out of the same position on electric with heavy tremolo. For the harmonized lines on the first and third strings, play fingerstyle or use hybrid picking, grabbing the lower note with a flatpick and the upper note with your middle finger.

Example 6 (à la "Fruits of My Labor")
Capo I

GHOST STORIES

While Williams' records have gravitated toward a gritty acoustic-electric sound, her songwriting always retains a connection to the acoustic folk she cut her teeth on. One notable example is "The Ghosts of Highway 20," the title track from her acclaimed 2016 album, reminiscent of traditional ballads by way of Bob Dylan.

Williams said the idea behind the song first came when she played a show back in Macon, which she found surprisingly unchanged from how she remembered it in the '50s. Leaving the city on the tour bus, she began thinking about how much of her childhood was strung along Highway 20. "Sometimes memories are like ghosts," she said. "They hang around and you can't get rid of them, and they torture you sometimes. You could think of it this way too: The blues artists who lived in those areas and are buried around there, they're literally blues ghosts, you know?"

Example 7 is based on the verse pattern in "The Ghosts of Highway 20" as she performs it live, in E minor (the album version is in D minor). Play a steady alternating bass throughout, over Em, C/G, and B7 shapes. Add treble notes sparingly with your fingers on the offbeats. On the B7, play along with the vocal melody as you go back to Em.

BACK TO THE WELL

Williams' 2020 album, *Good Souls Better Angels*, brings her full circle—right back to the sounds and themes of the gospel blues she heard Pearly Brown play on the street in Macon some 60 years ago.

Williams has always been drawn to religious language and imagery. "Both of my grandfathers were Methodist ministers, so that preaching thing was in my blood already," she said. "My dad wasn't a fundamentalist by any means, but I was still exposed to the hellfire, brimstone, and all the music that goes along with that. I was just intrigued by it, and I was also inspired by Southern writers like Flannery O'Connor and Eudora Welty, who wrote a lot about that small-town religious fanatic stuff."

Example 8 shows a sample of the rhythm pattern in "Pray the Devil Back to Hell," going between E7 and C/G with a capo at the third fret. Use a percussive slap on the backbeats marked with x and emphasize the bass, adding subtle hints of the underlying chords.

Example 7 (à la "The Ghosts of Highway 20")
No capo

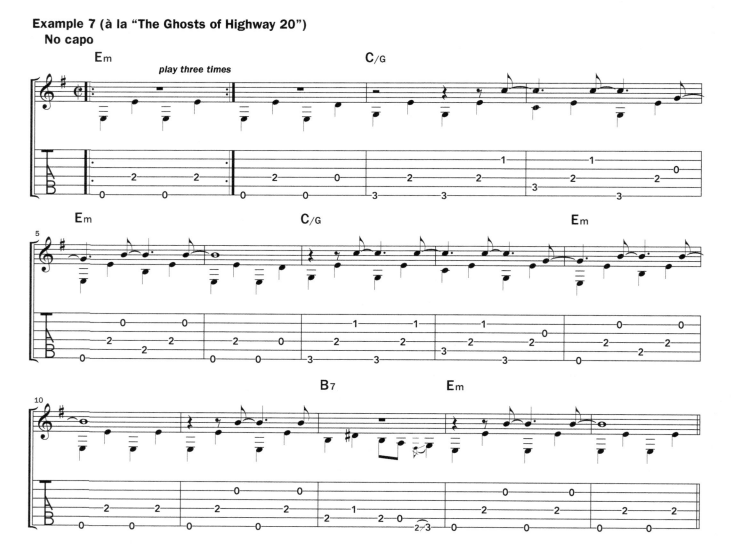

Also on *Good Souls Better Angels*, Williams revisits another early inspiration, Memphis Minnie, with a rewrite of Minnie's song "You Can't Rule Me." While the original song uses a I–IV–V progression, Williams strips it down to one basic chord, and her defiant lyrics take on political overtones.

Electric strumming drives "You Can't Rule Me" on the album; **Example 9** shows how Williams plays it acoustically (check out the duo performance she taped for *NPR*'s Tiny Desk). Alternate thumpy bass notes with slaps, like a kick and snare. In measures 2 and 4, do a quick slide up to the third fret on the low string.

With a voice deepened and weathered over the years, Williams has never come closer to the "dirty, guttural sound" she admired in Robert Johnson.

"It's kind of like what the Black Keys have been doing," she said. "I totally understood where they were coming from the first time I heard them, 'cause I knew they were channeling that Delta blues stuff. "It's just the best music. It comes from a place that's so deep and primitive and raw. There's nothing like it."

Example 8 (à la "Pray the Devil Back to Hell")
Capo III

Example 9 (à la "You Can't Rule Me")
Capo III

Acoustic Soul

Inside the Songs and Guitar Style of Bill Withers

By Jeffrey Pepper Rodgers

F ew artists have made such a deep imprint on the music world in such a short time as Bill Withers. He launched his music career relatively late—he was 32 when his debut album came out in 1971—and then walked away from it all within 15 years. And yet during that stretch of the '70s and early '80s, Withers delivered a string of classic songs, from "Ain't No Sunshine" and "Grandma's Hands" to "Lean on Me," "Lovely Day," and "Just the Two of Us," that continue to reverberate today. Built on the earthy grooves of his acoustic guitar, Withers' music drew on soul, blues, gospel, and country, but those genre distinctions seem irrelevant. With a rare gift for distilling an emotion or story down to its essence, Withers created songs that feel timeless and universal.

This feature originally appeared in the May/June 2021 issue of Acoustic Guitar *magazine.*

"He made such an enormous impact," says Son Little, whose own take on guitar-based R&B has drawn frequent comparisons to Withers. "I don't remember first hearing 'Lean on Me.' His songs have had such power and reach that they're really a part of the culture. It's true folk music."

Withers passed away in March 2020 from heart complications at age 81, prompting a fresh look at his musical legacy. While he always put the spotlight on his vocals and lyrics, one of the special features of Withers' music was his use of acoustic guitar—a rarity in the realm of soul/R&B, then and now. Withers himself was the first to point out that he was far from a fancy instrumentalist. "I can't play the guitar or the piano," he once told *The New York Times*, "but I made a career out of writing songs on guitars and piano." He developed a stripped-down accompaniment style that was the perfect vehicle for his songwriting, from gentle ballads to funked-up blues.

"He, more than anybody else, employed the acoustic guitar in R&B music in a really special way," Little says. "The songs break down easily into really simple patterns that you can play on an acoustic guitar. As with a lot of great music or art, its biggest strength is its simplicity."

Withers recognized that quality in his own work. "If you research it, very few songs that live in the minds of people are written by virtuoso musicians," he said in an interview with *American Songwriter*. "The things that they do are too complicated. There's an almost inverse ratio between virtuosity and popularity. Simplicity is directly related to availability for most people."

This lesson goes inside some of Withers' best songs—especially from his first few albums, when his own guitar was most prominent—to reveal the understated accompaniment style that carries them.

WORKINGMAN'S BLUES

Growing up, Withers hardly seemed headed for a life in music. Born and raised in the coal company town of Slab Fork, West Virginia, he did not play an instrument and, by his own account, had no special involvement with music as a child. Eager to escape working in the mines, as all the other men in his family had done, he joined the Navy at 17 and trained as an airline mechanic. Only in his late 20s, while working in an airline parts factory in California, did he pick up a pawnshop guitar and begin to write. Withers was still employed at the factory—installing toilets in 747s—when he was recording his debut album, as captured in the cover photo of Withers during a work break, lunch box in hand.

Signed to the Sussex label, Withers had the good fortune to be matched with producer Booker T. Jones, who chose to showcase Withers in his natural element on the aptly titled *Just As I Am*. Backed by Jones and his band, the MGs, with Stephen Stills subbing on guitar for Steve Cropper, Withers delivered an assured, soulful performance, with his acoustic guitar at the center of the mix.

The album's first single was the propulsive "Harlem," but the song that broke Withers' career wide open was its B side, "Ain't No Sunshine." Withers said the movie *The Days of Wine and Roses* inspired the lover's lament, which he set to a haunting melody over a minor blues progression. As it happened, Withers actually intended to write lyrics in place of the song's famous "I know" incantation, but Jones and the other session players convinced him to leave the ad lib in place.

Although "Ain't No Sunshine" is in A minor and could easily be played with open-position chord shapes, Withers rarely went that route on the guitar. Instead, he tended to reach for chord shapes up the neck, especially the types of three-note voicings often used in swing/jazz rhythm. So, in **Example 1**, grab the Am7 at the fifth fret. Play fingerstyle, picking the bass notes with your thumb and the upper notes with your index and middle fingers. Use open strings only on the

Example 1 (à la "Ain't No Sunshine")

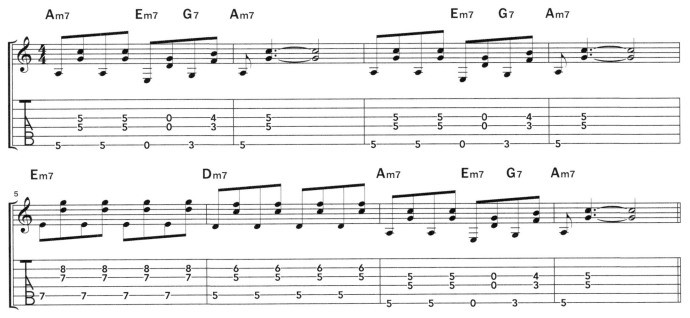

Em7 in measures 1 and 7 (for that chord, you don't need to fret any strings at all). The movable three-note shapes used for Am7, G7, Em7 (in measure 5), and Dm7 recur throughout Withers' music and the following examples.

Withers revisited his West Virginia childhood in "Grandma's Hands," another gem from his debut. His father died young, and Withers was raised primarily by his mother and grandmother. He credits his grandmother in particular as his early champion. "I was one of those kids who was smaller than all the girls; I stuttered, I had asthma, so I had some issues," Withers recalled in an interview at the Grammy Museum in 2014. "My grandmother was that one person who would always say that I was going to be OK." In "Grandma's Hands," he paid tribute through a series of vignettes of his grandmother, from playing the tambourine in church to helping an unwed mother to picking up young Billy when he fell.

Like "Ain't No Sunshine," "Grandma's Hands" uses a simple progression in a minor key, in this case E minor. In **Example 2**, on the Em, pick the sixth, fourth, and third strings simultaneously, adding the second fret on the third string on beat two to create the song's main riff. For the B7 and A7, hold the same shape you used for the G7 in "Ain't No Sunshine."

Example 2 (à la "Grandma's Hands")

SURPRISING PATTERNS

Withers' barebones approach on the guitar led him to some unusual places. One example is "I'm Her Daddy," a poignant track on *Just As I Am*, in which the narrator has discovered he has a six-year-old daughter. The song is in C♯ minor, a key that few folk guitarists would tackle without a capo. But that's exactly what Withers did, thanks to the closed chord shapes he favored. In **Example 3**, you actually do use the open sixth string as part of the bass line leading into the C♯m7 and F♯7. On these two chords, let the C♯ bass note (string 5, fret 4) ring while you pick the upper notes.

In the song's main rhythm pattern, the C♯ bass note falls not on the 1 but at the end of the previous measure—Withers often anticipated the downbeat in this way. This pattern has a sneaky variation, too, shown in measures 3 and 4. In measure 3, play the upper notes of the C♯m7 for one extra eighth note—that is, pick them six times rather than five, as before. This pushes the open string E to the last upbeat of the measure, so that the C♯ bass note then lands on the downbeat of measure 4.

If you listen closely to Withers' performance of "I'm Her Daddy" on *Just As I Am*, or the live takes from the early '70s available on YouTube, you'll hear him switch back and forth between these two variations throughout the song. In effect he is shifting by a half beat where the chord change falls—a cool detail that keeps the progression feeling slightly off balance. As you practice the example, keep time with your feet so you can feel the change and the syncopation.

Example 3 (à la "I'm Her Daddy")

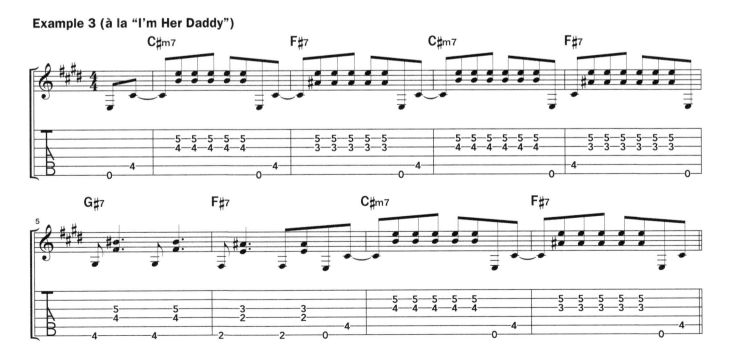

Also on his debut, the lonesome ballad "Hope She'll Be Happier" is built around the pattern in **Example 4**, played in the key of D using a fingering high up the neck. Fret the fifth string at the 12th fret for an A note above the root on the open fourth string; in measure 2, raise the fifth string to an A# for a Daug. Withers repeats this pattern for a long stretch before finally switching to Gm7, as shown in measure 5. The whole accompaniment part is as sparse as it could be, leaving nothing to distract from the emotion of Withers' vocal and story.

IN THE GROOVE

By late 1971, Withers' debut album vaulted him from the factory floor to the stage of *The Tonight Show*, as "Ain't No Sunshine" and "Grandma's Hands" rose on the charts. For performing, he found the perfect collaborators in the Los Angeles–based Watts 103rd Street Rhythm Band, who locked right into his less-is-more style. The antithesis of the showbiz front man, Withers held the stage with the band like a coffeehouse singer, seated with his flattop guitar even while laying down grooves that make it nearly impossible to stay off your feet.

The band was so tight that Withers managed to convince his label boss, Clarence Avant (profiled in the recent Netflix documentary *The Black Godfather*), to let him and the musicians self-produce his second studio album. That unusual freedom certainly paid off with 1972's *Still Bill*, chock-full of great songs and performances.

Two tracks on *Still Bill*, both based on two-chord vamps, serve as a good intro to how Withers played in a funk context. "Use Me," a hit on both the Hot 100 and soul charts, simply toggles between Em7 and A7, using the same minor seventh and dominant seventh shapes as "Ain't No Sunshine."

Example 4 (à la "Hope She'll Be Happier")

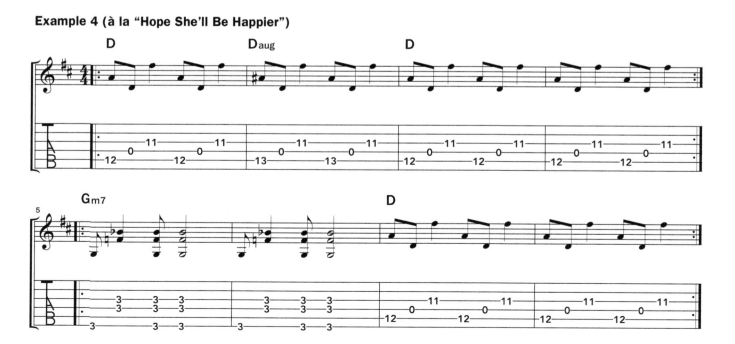

For **Example 5a**, grab a flatpick and get ready for a picking-arm workout—alternating down and up strums on every eighth note. On some beats, marked with X noteheads, relax your fretting fingers to get a percussive scratch instead of a chord. Even when you don't play, as on beat one of measure 4, keep the strum movement going—just bypass the strings. Hitting some open strings, as at the ends of measures 2 and 4, gives you a moment to change positions while maintaining the rhythm. In a passage like measure 4, which has mostly scratches, the guitar is essentially playing the role of maracas. To push the groove a little harder, emphasize the backbeats (2 and 4).

That insistent strum isn't designed to stand on its own, of course. Withers' groove-based songs have signature riffs overlaid as well. In "Use Me," Ray Jackson played a super funky repeating riff on clavinet; **Example 5b** shows a guitar adaptation. As with everything in Withers' music, the riff makes its mark while leaving lots of space. Avoid the temptation to noodle.

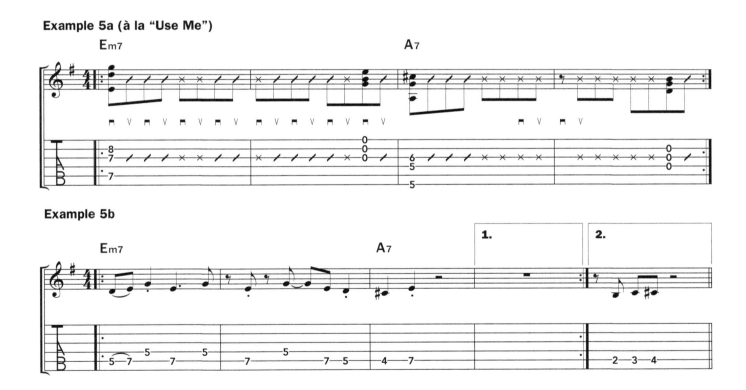

Example 5a (à la "Use Me")

Example 5b

The same instrumental dynamic holds in the opening track of *Still Bill*, "Lonely Town, Lonely Street." In **Example 6a**, again strum two chords, Bm7 and F♯m7, using the same three-note shape; maintain a down-up motion throughout, and mix chords with percussive scratches. Bear in mind that this is a loose, improvisational style, so the pattern shown is just one example—feel free to go with the flow and make your own variations. **Example 6b** then shows an accompanying riff, similar to what's played on the track on electric guitar (Benorce Blackmon) and bass (Melvin Dunlap).

Example 6a (à la "Lonely Town, Lonely Street")

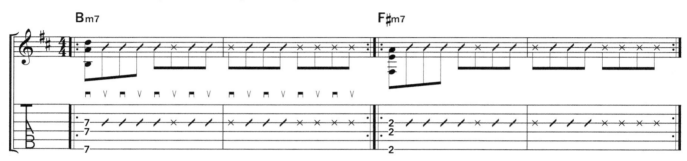

Example 6b

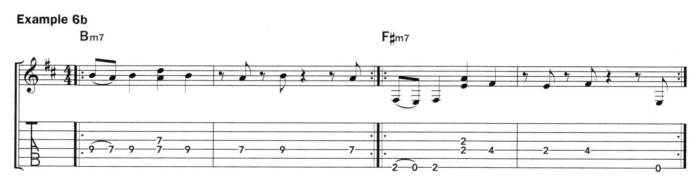

BEYOND THREE CHORDS

As the above examples demonstrate, Withers got an awful lot of songwriting mileage out of two- and three-chord progressions with just a few repeating chord shapes. But some of his songs use more complex progressions, especially collaborations such as the bossa nova–tinged "Hello Like Before" (written with John E. Collins and recorded with veteran session player Dennis Budimir on nylon-string guitar), "Lovely Day" (written with Skip Scarborough), and "Just the Two of Us" (written with William Salter and Ralph MacDonald, and first recorded by saxophonist Grover Washington Jr. with Withers as the featured singer). One early example of a song with more harmonic complexity, written by Withers alone and featuring his own guitar work, is the ballad "Let Me in Your Life" from *Still Bill*.

Example 7 is based on the introduction and part of the verse of "Let Me in Your Life," and opens with an F♯m7♭5 to F♯dim7 to Emaj7 progression that recurs later in the song. Play with your fingers, and for the repeating chords shown with a rhythm slash (as in measures 1, 5–7, etc.), strum with your thumb for a soft sound. Play the Emaj7 at the seventh fret, and in measures 4, 8, and 12, slide the shape up a fret for an Fmaj7 and then back down.

Example 7 (à la "Let Me in Your Life")

ON THE KEYS

In addition to his guitar-based music, Withers wrote plenty of songs on piano, and his later albums feature a much more keyboard-oriented, smooth R&B/pop sound. He wrote his most iconic song, "Lean on Me," on a Wurlitzer keyboard, following the simplest of patterns: starting on C, walking up the white keys (the major scale) to F, and walking back down. That line, harmonized, is the foundation of Withers' piano accompaniment and his melody. With its warm gospel sound and reassuring message of friendship, "Lean on Me" is a truly universal song, more resonant than ever during the social isolation of the pandemic.

To wrap up this tour of Withers' music, **Example 8** shows a guitar rendition of the simple idea immortalized in "Lean on Me." Play three- and four-note chords throughout, picking the individual strings with your fingers simultaneously for a sound closer to piano, as opposed to strumming. For the three-note chords, pick with your thumb, index, and middle fingers; for the four-note chords, employ your ring finger too. (Alternatively, you could pick all the three-note chords with your index, middle, and ring fingers, and bring in the thumb only for the four-note chords.) Note the fingering suggestions in measure 4, which will help you navigate the G6 to G9 and set you up for the return to C in the next measure.

THE RIGHT INTENT

It's remarkable that an artist with Withers' natural talents and popularity would opt out of a music career so early, releasing no new albums after 1985 and contributing to only a handful of songs recorded by other artists, such as "Simply Complicated" with Jimmy Buffett (2004) and "Mi Amigo Cubano" with Raul Midón (2014). Withers was more available to the public in recent years, especially through the 2009 documentary *Still Bill*—a must-watch for anyone interested in learning more about the man behind the music—and his induction into the Rock and Roll Hall of Fame in 2015. Deeply cynical about the music business and determined not to play what he termed the "fame game," Withers seemed very much at peace out of the spotlight.

Example 8 (à la "Lean on Me")

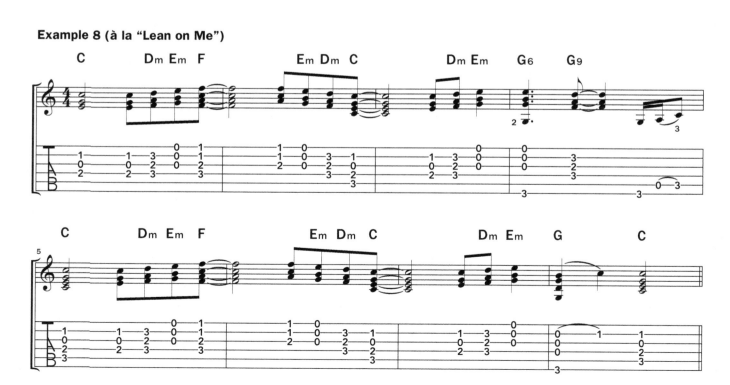

An immersion in Withers' music brings powerful lessons for any guitar-playing songwriter, especially about the value of directness. As a lyricist, he never got bogged down in cleverness or complicated metaphors. "Ain't no sunshine when she's gone." "Lean on me when you're not strong." Withers' words say what they mean and go straight to the emotional heart.

For Son Little, Withers' songs are a reminder that the guitar should not draw too much attention to itself. "If I'm thinking about your guitar playing, then you either messed up or you're playing too much," he says. "It's a hard lesson to learn—to trust the song, trust your voice. I'm still working on it."

Another musician I spoke with about Withers, Louisiana singer-songwriter and guitarist Marc Broussard, describes a similar revelation about his own approach to the instrument. "For a long time I felt it was necessary to get as technical and as clever as possible. I wanted the average listener to feel like it was just another song, but I wanted musicians to say, 'Oh, man, did you hear that modulation?' or 'Did you hear them go to that flat-five right there?' That was just a bunch of ego stroking.

"Then I started digging into Bill's stuff and realized that if you have the right intent, none of that is necessary. Two chords, three chords at the most sometimes; you just put the right melody and lyrics together, and everything else is just going to work itself out."

BILL WITHERS' GUITARS

Dreadnoughts were a good match for Bill Withers' muscular rhythm style, and concert footage from the 1970s shows him playing a Martin D-35 and a Gibson J-50—he appeared in Gibson ads around that time. Guitarists watching the *Still Bill* documentary may notice the array of instruments with unusual teardrop-shaped bodies behind Withers in some interview segments. These are Craviola guitars, originally designed in the late '60s by guitarist/composer Paulinho Nogueira and built by the Brazilian company Giannini. Jimmy Page famously played a 12-string Craviola in the early '70s on Led Zeppelin's "Tangerine." Giannini still builds a Craviola line that includes steel- and nylon-string acoustics, electrics, and basses. —*Jeffrey Pepper Rodgers*

PICTORIAL PRESS LTD / ALAMY STOCK PHOTO

Gold Tones

Learn Neil Young's Simple and Singular Style

By Adam Levy

Some guitarists search obsessively for novel chord voicings to spice up their songs or arrangements. While there's nothing wrong with such predilections, it's easy to overlook the fact that there's already quite a bit of variety available within the everyday open-position chords—G, Am, D, and so on.

These static forms can easily be made livelier by momentarily adding or subtracting a finger. While chords built this way may have overly complicated names—Cmaj7(add2), for example, which is just a standard C shape with the first and second fingers lifted—such ostentatious tags belie the simple moves that lead to their construction.

Among the many players who've used such tactics to create sui generis riffs and chord progressions, perhaps

no one has been more successful than Neil Young, the prolific singer-songwriter responsible for "Heart of Gold," "The Needle and the Damage Done," "Harvest Moon," and dozens of other folk-rock classics.

In this lesson, you'll examine some of Young's renowned handiwork, as well as some of the lesser-known songs from his catalog. The examples here were mostly inspired by the guitarist's work from the early to mid-1970s—a particularly fertile period for him. The

This feature originally appeared in the October 2017 issue of Acoustic Guitar *magazine.*

hallmarks of his guitar style can all be found on his records from this era, made and released when he was approaching 30 years of age.

Two albums that showcase Young's style in a stripped-down setting—his voice, his guitar, and nothing more—are *Live at Massey Hall* (recorded onstage in 1971, released in 2007) and the "lost" album *Hitchhiker* (recorded live in the studio in 1976). Both of these earlyish recordings feature many songs that would go on to become staples of Young's concert repertoire, and both offer ample opportunity to examine his guitar style more closely.

COME TO G(SUS)

There are a few ways to finger the familiar G chord. **Example 1a** shows one common choice, employing fingers 1, 2, and 3. Young tends to favor an alternate grip (**Example 1b**), with fingers 2, 3, and 4. Out of context, there may not seem to be much difference between the two. Young's preference makes sense, however, when you begin to study how he uses that freed first finger to add harmonic variety to the G chord—as you'll see in the examples to follow.

The spartan, Young-approved G form you'll be using in **Example 1c** allows even more harmonic latitude—muting the

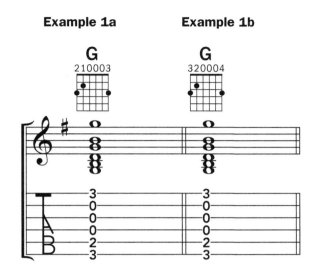

fifth string and leaving the first and second fingers unfettered. This example is loosely based on Young's wispy intro and verse figure from "Through My Sails," the last track on his 1975 album *Zuma*. The four-measure phrase is built upon I–vi–IV–V—one of those ubiquitous chord progressions in popular music.

Example 1c (à la "Through My Sails")

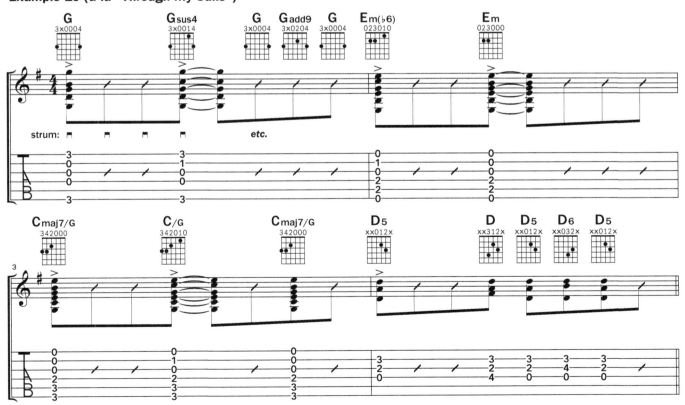

This example is in the key of G major, as is Young's original, so the progression here is G–Em–C–D. Remember to fret the G chord with your third and fourth fingers. Keep this shape held in place when you switch to the Gsus4 and Gadd9 chords. Similarly, play the Em chord with your second and third fingers, leaving your first finger free to form the Em(♭6) chord in measure 2; play Cmaj7/G with fingers 2, 3, and 4, so that you can easily convert it to Cmaj7/G by adding your first finger on the second string. In measure 4, be careful not to sound the first string. Keep these fingering concepts in mind when playing **Example 1d**, inspired by the chorus of "Through My Sails."

Example 1d

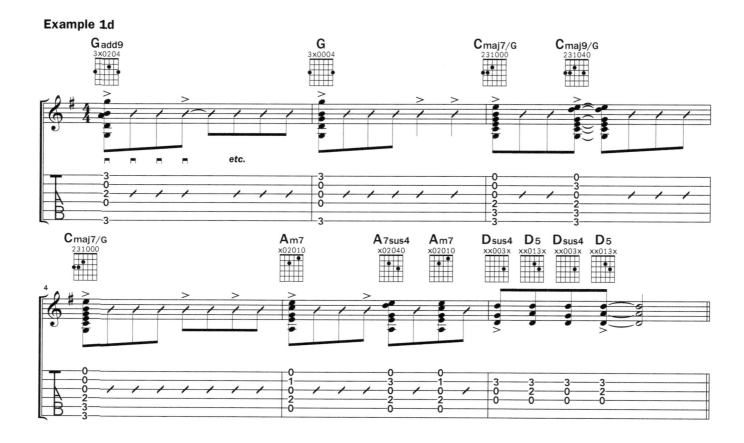

BEACH MUSIC

Example 2a is inspired by Young's electric-guitar intro to "Revolution Blues," from his 1974 album *On the Beach*. Here, a static Am chord is enlivened with simple adjustments. The addition of the fourth finger converts Am to Asus4. Lifting the second and third fingers gives you Am11. That said, such a freeze-frame view of the harmony only tells half the story. The other thing that's going on here is that such moves add melodic interest. You could— and should—try a similar approach to other basic chords, as shown in **Examples 2b–d**. In these four examples, play the first eighth note in each measure by muting the strings with your fretting hand. Don't press too hard. The resulting sound should be percussive, with no particular pitch.

Examples 2a–d (à la "Revolution Blues")

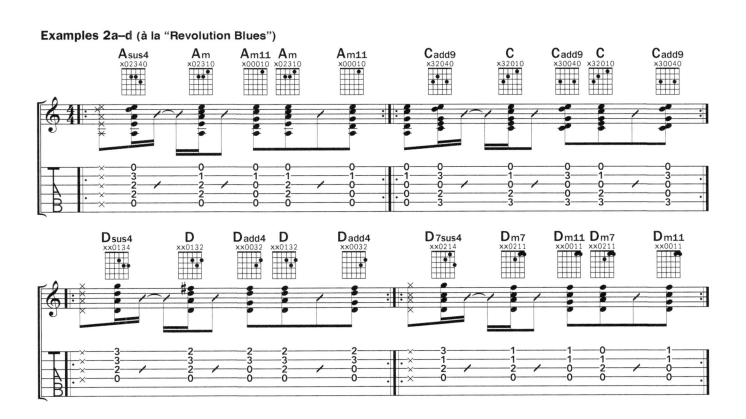

Example 3 is modeled on the intro from another *On the Beach* song—"Motion Pictures (for Carrie)." Here, you'll be using a whole-step-down variant of standard tuning (low to high: D G C F A D). As such, what looks like a D chord will sound like a C chord, and so on. This slackened tuning drenches the entire song in a swampy, slow-mo atmosphere.

In measure 1, an incremental change transforms the D chord to Dmaj7. You might expect that descending line on string 2, from D to C♯, to keep going down so that the next chord is D7. That does in fact happen, but the chord is given a fresh spin through the fleeting appearance of the chord's fourth/11th, G. On beats 1 and 3, hammer on the third string from open to fret 2. These hammers-ons are meant to be played in time, as 16th notes, so don't just hammer as quickly as you can. Make sure to feel that rhythm as you play. Also take heed of the accented beats. These give Ex. 3 a particularly Youngian swagger.

SHAPE SHIFTING

Besides amending common chords, another simple yet effective technique that Young uses in several songs is moving a single, non-barre shape up the fretboard to change its character while open-string notes sustain above and/or below the fretted notes. This is particularly effective in double-drop-D tuning (D A D G B D, sometimes called D modal). A good example of this is "Old Laughing Lady," from *Neil Young*, originally released in 1969.

Example 3 (à la "Motion Pictures [for Carrie]")
Tuning: D G C F A D

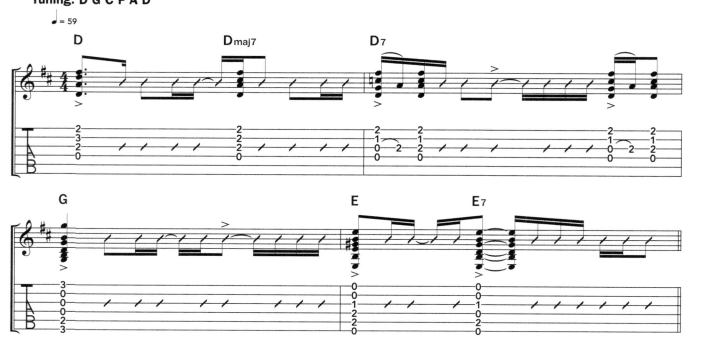

Example 4a is modeled on the first two measures of "Old Laughing Lady." No shifting-shape technique just yet. Instead, this two-bar phrase is similar to the examples you've already seen in this lesson, where chords are modified by adding or subtracting fingers. In this case, D5 becomes Dsus4. This example illustrates the kinds of sound that D-modal tuning is so perfect for. Notice how rich the D-type chords sound as the open first and sixth strings ring out.

In **Example 4b**, based on the song's verse chords, you can see how a simple two-finger shape—the D5 in measure 1—is subsequently used to make D6/9, Dmaj7, and Dsus4 chords. Conceptually, this is not unlike the single-shape chord sequence Young used for the verse chords of "Don't Let It Bring You Down," from *After the Gold Rush*, released in 1970. Young employed a similar tuning for that song, with all six strings dropped an additional whole step (C G C F A C).

Example 4a (à la "Old Laughing Lady")
Tuning: D A D G B D

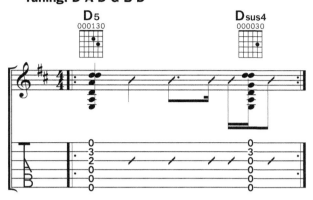

Example 4b

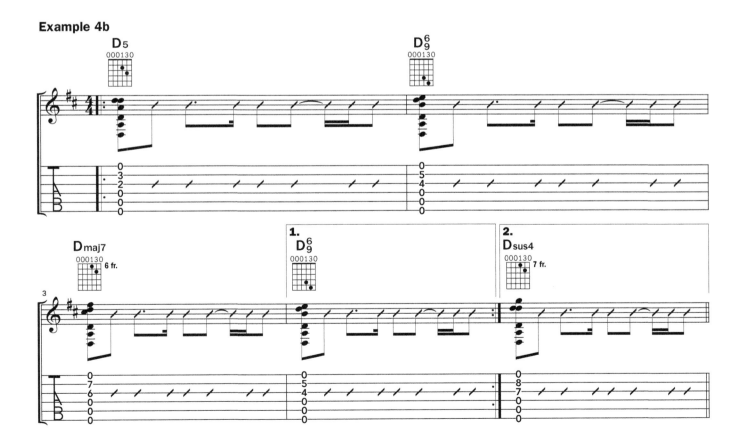

Use this low variation of the modal tuning for **Example 4c**, based on the verse chords for "Don't Let It Bring You Down." Here, a D5 grip (measures 1 and 2) is shifted up three frets and reused as Dm7 (measures 3 and 4), then moved two frets higher to make Dsus4 (measures 5 and 6), before finally being abandoned for other chord forms (measures 7 and 8). Play the 16ths here with a slight swing feel, as Young does on his original recording. In such an asymmetrical groove, the down-strummed 16th notes should last just a tiny bit longer than their up-strummed counterparts. Experiment with the down-up ratio until it feels authentically Young-like.

Example 4c
Tuning: C G C F A C

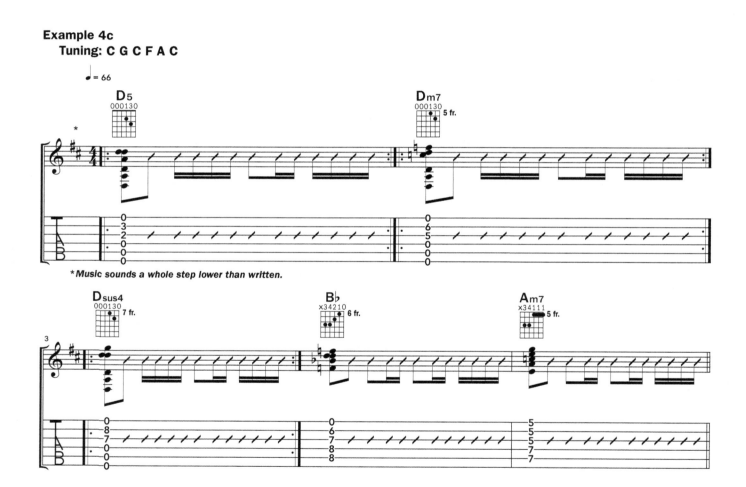

*Music sounds a whole step lower than written.

BEGGING YOUR PARDON

Example 5 is kindred with the intro to "Pardon My Heart," from *Zuma*. The tuning here is drop D, down a whole step. If you're still in the "Don't Let It Bring You Down" tuning, simply raise your first string up a whole step. The picking-hand technique for this example is more closely related to clawhammer banjo technique than to typical guitar strumming or fingerpicking patterns. Begin with your hand in a loose fist. Strike each down-stemmed bass note with your thumb, then feather the up-stemmed chords with your fingers by opening and closing your fist in the appropriate rhythms. (This technique will already be familiar to those of you who know how to play John Mayer's "Stop this Train.")

As with the hammer-ons you played in Ex. 3, the hammers here (on beat 3 of measures 1 and 3, and on beat 1 of measure 2) are key to making this feel authentically Young-like. Be sure to play them in time, and with enough force to match the dynamics of the non-hammered notes here. If it takes you awhile to get this groove to actually feel groovy, don't despair. It's not easy, but definitely worth the effort.

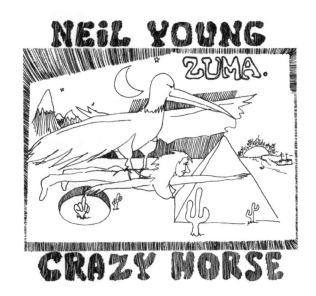

Example 5 (à la "Pardon My Heart")
Tuning: C G C F A D

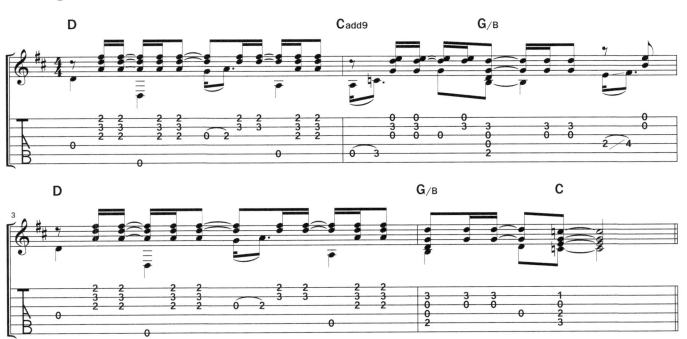

BACK TO BASICS

This lesson's final two examples are in standard tuning and both are meant to be played with a pick. After spending some time in Young's low-down alternate tunings, you may find that standard tuning feels fresh to your ears and hands once again. **Example 6** has echoes of "Look Out for My Love," from the 1978 album *Comes a Time*. Once again, the elements here are simple and familiar, but are assembled in a distinctive way. In measure 1, the top-line melody adds the ninth (F♯) of the E5 chord on beat 3. A similar move happens two measures later, where A briefly turns to Asus4.

While the rhythms here are meant to be played as written, a quarter-note pulse should be ghosted throughout. (If you're not sure what this means, listen to Young's original recording.) Bring your strumming hand down on each quarter—hitting the strings a little harder when there's a specific bass note to play (as in measure 1, beat 1) and a little lighter when there's not (measure 1, beats 2 and 3). You'll catch the chords and melodic flourishes (all up-stemmed) with the same pendular motion—using downstrokes for any downbeat notes, upstrokes for any upbeat notes.

"Heart of Gold," from Young's 1972 album, *Harvest*, is the inspiration for **Example 7**.

Like your first couple of examples here, Ex. 7 uses common chords—Em7, D, and Em—to build a mighty riff. Part of what gives this sequence its rugged feel is the lone bass note sounded on the downbeats of measures 1 and 3, immediately followed by a slew of unrelenting eighths. Another powerful factor here is the hammered melodic line—built from the E minor pentatonic scale (E G A B D)—at the ends of measures 2 and 4. Rocket science? No. Folk-rock gold? Yes.   **AG**

Example 6 (à la "Look Out for My Love")

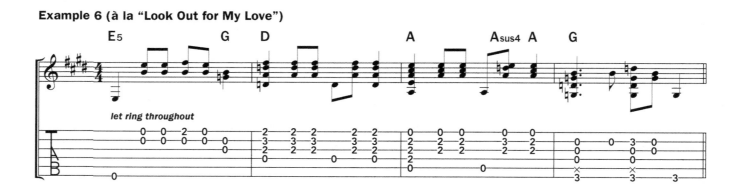

Example 7 (à la "Heart of Gold")

About the Authors

 Adam Levy is an itinerant guitarist based in Brooklyn, New York. His work has appeared on recordings by Norah Jones, Lisa Loeb, Amos Lee, and Ani DiFranco, among others. He is also the founder of Guitar Tips Pro. *guitartipspro.com*

 Adam Perlmutter, the editor of *Acoustic Guitar* magazine, is a graduate of the Contemporary Improvisation program at the New England Conservatory of Music.

 **Mac Randall**, editor of *JazzTimes* magazine and author of *Exit Music: The Radiohead Story*, has been playing guitar for 40 years and writing about music and related subjects for more than 30. *macrandallwriter.com*

 Jeffrey Pepper Rodgers, the founding editor of *Acoustic Guitar* and current editor at large, is a guitarist and singer-songwriter based in upstate New York. *jeffreypepperrodgers.com*

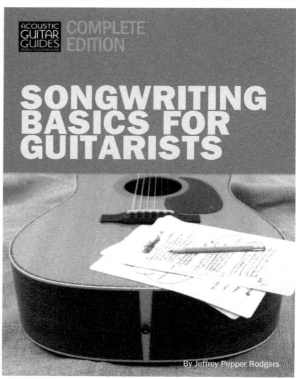

Subscribe to *Acoustic Guitar* Magazine

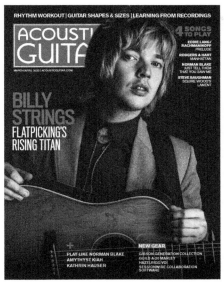

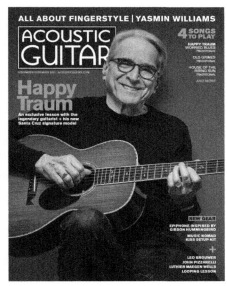

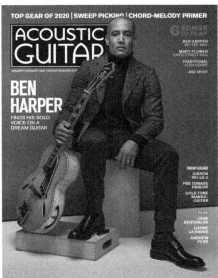

Every issue of *Acoustic Guitar* features full tab, notation, performance notes, and background on at least 5 songs, from classic rock and pop hits to campfire favorites, jazz, fingerstyle, flatpicking, and beyond, with music for players at all skill levels. Plus in-depth conversations with today's guitarists, practical advice on evaluating, buying, and caring for instruments and gear, and insights into the rich heritage of the guitar.

Get 1 year for ~~$47.94~~ $29.99!

While you're at it: Score 70% off music notation and TAB for more than 1,475 great songs. The *Acoustic Guitar* Digital Archive grants you instant access to these songs, plus interviews with guitar legends, lessons with trailblazing players, and so much more.

subscribe today at store.AcousticGuitar.com